Memories of DOWNTOWN BIRMINGHAM

Memories of DOWNTOWN BIRMINGHAM

WHERE ALL THE LIGHTS WERE BRIGHT

TIM HOLLIS

THE History PRESS

Published by The History Press
Charleston, SC 29403
www.historypress.net

All images are courtesy of the author's collection unless otherwise noted.

Cover image: Third Avenue North was probably the most visually spectacular section of Birmingham's downtown retail and theater district, and the photographer who captured this stunning image apparently had the good fortune to do so while the street was still wet from a recent rain.

First published 2014

Manufactured in the United States

ISBN 978.1.62619.221.8

Library of Congress CIP data applied for.

Much of what people remember fondly about downtown Birmingham could be found on Second Avenue North, the subject of this 1960s aerial view. Look closely, and you will find the Ritz Theater, the New Ideal store and the cluster of businesses that nestled underneath the small parking deck at the corner of Eighteenth Street and Second Avenue.

CONTENTS

INTRODUCTION

It might be a good idea, here at the outset, to explain a little about how this book came about and what it is intended to do. First, the original manuscript was cobbled together almost ten years ago. That version was never published, although it did form the basis for the photos- and captions-only collection released in the spring of 2005 as *Birmingham's Theater and Retail District*. That long delay in its publication has actually worked in its favor; as you will see, the final chapter of this book, had it appeared when first written, would have had an exceedingly melancholy ending. Fortunately, what we have here ends in a much more upbeat mood.

The title, *Memories of Downtown Birmingham*, has multilayered significance. While trying to decide what businesses (stores, theaters, restaurants) to include, precedence had to be given to those most likely to be remembered by people who are still alive. There were scores of these that existed in the city's earliest days but whose names are known only to local historians. Did you ever shop at Caheen Brothers or the L.F.M. Store, or attend a show at O'Brien's Opera House? I didn't think so. Such pioneering enterprises are not totally ignored but are somewhat shoved to the background in favor of their more famous descendants.

Funny thing about memories, they can be good, or they can be bad, sometimes simultaneously. That is the paradox that inevitably arises whenever one contrasts the golden age of downtown Birmingham with the era of segregation it came to exemplify (and, ironically, eventually helped to end). Similar to the case of the early businesses, this is a topic dealt with only insofar as it relates to the story being told. As newspaper writers have documented in later years, even those for whom downtown meant separate restrooms and drinking fountains—and who didn't dare even think of eating at one of the department store lunch counters—still have some warm memories of the neighborhood, too. Civil rights icon Abraham Woods went on record as saying that, as abhorrent as the customs of segregation had been, he still enjoyed shopping in the stores to the extent it was permissible. In 1994, Woods told a *Birmingham News* reporter, "I look at downtown today and see all those empty buildings, and I am saddened…I think of how it used to be with all the people going to and fro."

One thing Woods and everyone else could enjoy, regardless of their race, were the spectacular Christmas displays and celebrations that took place downtown. Those are conspicuous by their absence in this book, but for a good reason. The story of Christmas in Birmingham is such a good one that it deserves a book of its own, which is exactly the plan. For now, just think of that one as a present that still lies beneath your tree, waiting to be unwrapped in some future Yuletide season.

Now that all of these facts have been established, we need to begin with what we might consider the "prehistoric" part of the story. The city of Birmingham did not exist, not even as a village, until late 1871. Until then, its future site was a wooded acreage known as Jones Valley. A few miles to the west sat the community of Elyton, where a land company was organized specifically to buy up property in Jones Valley and build the city that would be known as Birmingham (after the British city of the same name, but with a different pronunciation). The fact that Birmingham was laid out in such an orderly fashion—with sequentially numbered streets crossing similarly numbered avenues—can be attributed to the fact that it was all drawn out on paper before any property was sold. As it turned out, that initial land sale was at the corner of First Avenue and Nineteenth Street, and it was a store that was built on the spot.

Once Birmingham was well and truly established, it took several years for it to attract any businesses of the type that would come to be associated with the downtown area. In the early days, Birmingham was often compared to a Wild West mining town, with unsavory characters and even more unsavory business establishments in profusion. By ten or fifteen years after the city's birth, however, there began to be signs that it could better itself, and that is where our story begins.

Chapter 1

CLASH OF THE TITANS

Anyone who brings up the subject of downtown department stores will immediately be confronted by the names of the two battling biggies of that genre: Loveman's and Pizitz. Now, if you are interested in these two retail giants, you will be happy to know that their complete histories have been told in books of their own: *Pizitz: Your Store* (2010) and *Loveman's: Meet Me Under the Clock* (2012). Rather than trying to condense two full-length books into a few pages, here I shall simply summarize the stories of these venerable mercantile establishments.

Adolph B. Loveman was a former shepherd from Hungary who immigrated to the United States to make a better life for himself as a merchant. In 1870, he opened a small store in Greensboro, Alabama, and by 1887 saw enough promise in the sixteen-year-old Birmingham to move his business there. Over the next few years, he took on two partners—Moses V. Joseph and Emil Loeb—and the name of the business became Loveman, Joseph & Loeb.

The original Loveman store in Birmingham was located on Second Avenue, but in 1890, the firm bought a piece of property at the corner of Third Avenue and Nineteenth Street that would end up being its home for the next ninety years. Between 1890 and 1900, the building continued to grow and expand until it occupied almost a quarter of that entire city block.

Very little is known about Adolph Loveman's early life, and he died in 1916, well before any historic interest in his store came about. The merchant who would become Loveman's most erstwhile competitor, however, had a well-documented career. In the 1950s, Louis Pizitz was inspired to write down his memories of the past, and he was very specific in describing his more-than-humble beginnings. Born in Poland in 1867, Pizitz worked at a variety of business ventures in his home country, some of which prospered, while others failed. He ultimately left Poland for the United States and recalled:

> *When I reached New York, I did not have a dollar and walked around the streets for three days, sleeping in the park and eating garbage on the streets. I met up with a Mrs. Frank from Augusta, Georgia. She was from my same town in Poland, so she wanted to help me. She said she had peddlers' supplies of goods in Augusta, and took me home with her and gave me some jewelry to peddle. I carried a pack on my back for two and one-half years. In this time I saved up $750.*

With the money he had saved, Pizitz opened a small store in Swainsboro, Georgia, but his wife convinced him he would do better in a large city—one like, say, Birmingham. "At that time Ferd Marx was on the corner where my store is today. He moved over to a store next door to the Caheen Brothers, and I took over the corner and paid $100 a month rent. I stayed there two months and did nothing. I was disgusted and wanted to go back to Swainsboro, but my wife insisted that I keep trying."

Finally, Pizitz hit on an idea. He began to sell his merchandise for a few cents less than any of the other stores, and this helped him establish his reputation as the store for the common man. Before too long, he had made enough money to begin buying up the other buildings on his block, giving the store room to expand. What we all know as the Pizitz store building was completed by 1925. From that point on, Pizitz and Loveman's would continue to glare at each other from their respective corners.

Even though the two bloomed into carbon copies of each other, at least at this point in time, Pizitz was still considered the store for the less well-to-do. A.B. Loveman's son Joseph had succeeded the ex-shepherd as head of the store, but in the mid-1920s, it was sold to a New Jersey company, City Stores. The Loveman family continued to be involved in the day-to-day operations, but the business's ultimate ownership by City Stores would prove to have some unwanted consequences in the future.

With the Great Depression making one giant poorhouse out of Alabama—which, of course, was not one of the more prosperous states in the first place—Louis Pizitz found himself doing more and more

The Pizitz department store building was constructed in two separate phases between 1923 and 1925. In this view from 1949, the venerable retail establishment was celebrating its fiftieth anniversary by replacing the customary "Your Store" slogan with a "Golden Year" theme.

philanthropic work for the hard-hit citizens of Birmingham. As for Loveman's, the turning point during the Depression was not its charitable work, but the event that took place on the afternoon of March 10, 1934. On that date, someone noticed smoke coming from Loveman's sub-basement, a four-foot-high crawl space below the building's actual basement. The cramped quarters made firefighting difficult, but soon, the firemen thought they had extinguished the small conflagration.

Upstairs, customers and staff members had been evacuated with no difficulties, and by 2:00 p.m., Joseph Loveman was telling the media that he planned to reopen the store as soon as he was given the all-clear signal. That signal would not come for another year and a half—at least not on that site. An hour later, flames that had crept to the upper floors undetected, traveling through the space between the inner and outer walls, exploded violently. As historian Jerry Laughlin later wrote, "The store was like a huge matchbox waiting for a spark. The heated wooden floors burst into flames, rapidly

The original Loveman, Joseph & Loeb department store building, the biggest part of which was completed in 1899, burned into nothingness in March 1934. At the far right-hand side of this shot, we can barely see the "Loeb" remnant of the vertical sign, most of which had already collapsed into the foreground by this point.

leaping upward…Jagged tongues of flame poured out of every window. In ten incredible minutes the fire leapfrogged throughout the building." When the walls and roof collapsed like a burning deck of cards, everyone knew Loveman's was finished.

Within days, Joseph Loveman made arrangements to reopen in the large building at the corner of Third Avenue and Eighteenth Street that had been vacated by its original owner, Parisian, just a year or so earlier. By that summer, plans had been unveiled for the new Loveman's, and after a little over a year's construction time, the gleaming white limestone four-story edifice rose, phoenix-like, from the ashes of the original structure. No effort was spared to make it the most lavish, modern store in Alabama. Of great wonder to all was the escalator—the first in Birmingham—that ran from the first to second floors.

Oh, and of course, let us not forget the new Loveman's most distinguishing characteristic—in fact, one of the true landmarks in all of downtown. The

The gleaming new art deco–style Loveman's building (the name was shortened during the postwar days) opened in November 1935. As seen in this 1947 shot, it served as a proud neighbor to the magnificent Alabama Theatre.

flattened corner at Third Avenue and Nineteenth Street was decorated with a large clock that became famous not so much as a timepiece but as a convenient meeting place for those who were lost or otherwise needed a point of reference. "Meet me under the clock at Loveman's" became as familiar a phrase in Birmingham as "Roll Tide" or "I see Vulcan's torch is red tonight."

Of course, even though he was a proven good guy, Louis Pizitz probably gritted his teeth a bit at the attention his competition's lavish new store was getting. Nothing much was done about it, though, until after World War II was out of the way. In 1948, Pizitz did Loveman's one better by installing escalators from the first to fourth floors, with native Birmingham movie and Broadway star Mary (Bebe) Daniels on hand for the ribbon cutting. Loveman's retaliated in 1955 by installing its own escalators to every floor, from the basement up.

Joseph Loveman died in 1951, and Louis Pizitz followed in 1959. Loveman's would continue to be run by various successors appointed by City Stores, but Pizitz remained in the family, initially under the control of Louis's son, Isadore. These "next generation" businesspeople were the ones on hand to witness the changes that would alter their stores' futures forever.

Del Chambordon, who worked at Loveman's for its last thirty-eight years of business, had been a customer since childhood, and she remarked that no one would even think of entering Loveman's, Pizitz or any of the other downtown stores without being properly dressed. "Your shoes were polished, your hair was combed, and you had a hair bow or ribbon and a pocketbook," she said. "You held your mother's hand, and you knew how to behave." David Vann, later mayor of Birmingham, recalled an incident from his teenage days when he accompanied his aunt on a shopping trip but was made to sit in the car because he was wearing moccasins, hardly proper attire for visiting a downtown store. Such pride was attached to the stores that later Loveman's president Jerry Sklar remembers that people would take empty Loveman's boxes and bags and use them to give less expensive presents that had been purchased somewhere else. Just that elegant logo, with its gracefully scripted initial *L*, was enough to say quality.

Pizitz had much the same reputation, and as stated earlier, by the 1950s, it was difficult to tell the two stores apart. Del Chambordon insisted that the rivalry was always kept civil, and no Loveman's employee risked being fired if he or she were caught visiting Pizitz, for example. "Where the competition got dead serious," she said, "was in the buying and merchandising. If Pizitz got in some new item we did not have at Loveman's, the buyer for that department would be called in to the office and severely questioned as to why they did not make that particular purchase. Neither store wanted the other to outdo [it]."

Of course, competition is usually a good thing since it inspires businesses to be constantly improving themselves in order to keep up with each other. In 1965, Pizitz scored some more points by opening its multilevel parking deck at the corner of First Avenue and Eighteenth Street. A "skywalk," or

Pizitz had established its initial reputation as a store for the common folk, but by the 1960s, it was just as upscale as competitor Loveman's. Here, we see WBRC-TV's stunningly beautiful Pat Gray strutting her stuff for Pizitz at an in-store fashion show. *Pat Gray collection.*

suspended walkway, connected the parking deck to the third floor of the Pizitz store. After leaving the parking deck and entering the store, the first sight that greeted shoppers was Pizitz's baked goods counter, with an aroma of fresh cookies and candy that was enough to stop hundreds of people dead in their tracks before proceeding. Loveman's followed by opening its own parking deck in 1971, replacing an earlier two-story structure that was woefully inadequate.

It looked as though Pizitz and Loveman's would always be around to keep each other on their toes. However, trouble began to loom for Loveman's that was even more devastating and permanent than the 1934 fire. In 1979, City Stores filed for bankruptcy. The company continued operating its various department store chains around the country but launched an effort to sell off the least profitable ones.

By that time, Loveman's had six stores in Alabama, and all were doing relatively well, except the old original downtown location. It was beginning to be obvious that the huge dinosaur was weighing down the possibility of getting the others out of debt. When the end finally came, it was quick, if not exactly painless. On April 2, 1980, president Jerry Sklar held a press conference to announce that in three days, all six Loveman's stores would close forever. "I would do anything in the world to change the situation as far as Loveman's is concerned," he told reporters. "It is a great company and a great name."

In December 1986, the Pizitz family announced that they would sell their thirteen-store chain, including the downtown store, to Jackson, Mississippi's McRae's chain. Business would continue pretty much as usual under the McRae's name, and if not for the change in signage, many people might not have even realized that Pizitz was no more. In fact, far more media attention was garnered by McRae's announcement in February 1988 that it would close the downtown store because of its lack of profitability. Longtime customers reacted as though Pizitz itself were closing, when in fact that event had taken place a year and two months earlier.

Isadore Pizitz's three sons, Richard, Merritt and Michael, had no intention of getting out of the retail business just because their family name was no longer on public display. To this day, they continue to operate diverse interests, including the Gus Mayer department store. There is even a Louis Pizitz Middle School in Vestavia, an honor not bestowed on any of the other veteran downtown retailers.

Chapter 2

SOONER OR LATER, YOUR FAVORITE STORES

Of course, there were plenty of other stores downtown besides Pizitz and Loveman's. The rest fell into more specialized categories, such as clothiers and variety or "five and ten" stores, which catered to a different group of people than did the elegant department stores.

In the former group was Blach's, long known as the source for high-quality clothing. The complete history of this downtown landmark can be found in James Bennett's comprehensive book *Blach's: The Store, the Family, Their Story* (2013), but I can point out a few highlights here. Like Louis Pizitz and Adolph Loveman, Julius Blach was an immigrant who crossed the Atlantic from his native Germany to seek a better life. He eventually settled in Vevey, Indiana, and opened his first store there in 1856.

The official name of the business was J. Blach and Sons, and it was more than fitting. Because Julius had seven sons (not to mention his six daughters), he was able to establish additional stores in Nashville, Tennessee; Louisville, Kentucky; Cincinnati, Ohio; and Springfield, Missouri. In 1885, son Simon opened a Birmingham store that would come to be the main focus for the family.

Once the Blachs came to Birmingham, they set up operations in a variety of locations, most of which were along First Avenue North. One thing remained constant among all of them, and that was the Blach's emblem of a lily and a carpenter's square, visual shorthand for the store's motto: "Fair and Square." One Birmingham newspaper elaborated on the multiple meanings of this logo:

> *First you see the circle, indicative of* [the] *endless power of good within. Second, you see the lily, indicative of purity. Third, you see the green leaf, indicative of everlasting life. Fourth, you see the square, indicative of true dealing. Then taking the lily in its fair whiteness and combining it with the square, you produce that well-known motto of this firm—Fair and Square—which has not a blot of unjust dealing against it.*

Blach's was unique among the locally owned Birmingham stores in that the "Fair and Square" emblem was registered as a trademark with the U.S. Patent Office in 1892. In one form or another, this logo and slogan would remain with the store for the next century.

Quickly outgrowing available space, in 1905, Blach's moved to the corner of Third Avenue and Nineteenth Street. Family lore tells how, at the time, this was considered so far from the main retail district that Blach's hired a band to play on its uppermost floor to attract shoppers from First and Second Avenues. Once the customers found the store, it prospered beyond all expectations; photos of the building show an incredible electrical spectacular of a sign on the corner, with the lily and carpenter's square fashioned from dozens of light bulbs.

In 1935, the property on which the store sat was leased for the new S.H. Kress store (more on this store later). Blach's simply picked up stakes and suits and moved to the other end of the block, opening in June 1936. Its new building at the corner of Third and Twentieth had formerly been the Bencor Hotel and had to undergo some major remodeling to be converted into a store.

Eventually branch stores were opened at Eastwood Mall, Mountain Brook, Brookwood Village and Huntsville, but the flagship downtown store closed in 1984. Actually, it did not officially close so much as simply change locations. Later in this book, we will encounter the unfortunate story of Costa and Head and how that partnership's attempt to revive downtown in the early 1980s almost destroyed priceless historical treasures. One of the few Costa-Head projects that actually got completed was the construction of an atrium in the space between the Kress and Burger-Phillips buildings. This is where Blach's moved its downtown location, which, despite being dramatically downsized, managed to hang on until March 1988.

It should be obvious by now that the late 1800s was a prime time for European immigrants to set up their own businesses in America. To the list of those who became integral parts of downtown Birmingham's fabric I should add Jacob Burger, who founded the Burger Dry Goods Company

In 1936, the Bencor Hotel was remodeled as the new home of the long-established Blach's department store. When this photo was made, some of the hotel's exterior signage was still visible, although Blach's was using as much space as possible to advertise its upper-class wares.

An unidentified photographer captured this amazing view of Third Avenue North at dusk in the late 1940s. We are standing on the corner of Twentieth Street and looking west, taking in Blach's, Kessler's, S.H. Kress and other stores all the way to the Birmingham Theater (formerly the Pantages) at Seventeenth Street.

on Second Avenue in 1895. Despite the store's name, Jacob Burger had two (silent?) partners, brothers Ignatz and Louis Phillips. Belatedly rectifying the oversight, in 1923 the name of the store was changed to Burger-Phillips.

When growth caused the store to look for larger quarters, an ambitious plan was launched. The corner of Second Avenue and Eighteenth Street

After beginning life on Second Avenue, Burger-Phillips moved to more luxurious digs on Third Avenue in 1933. By 1937, the store had been joined by Blach's at one end of the block and S.H. Kress on the other. *Birmingham, Alabama Public Library Archives, Catalogue #820.11.1.*

had long been occupied by the Birmingham post office. That venerable old building was sitting unused when Burger-Phillips purchased the property and announced its intention to build an incredible ten-story structure to house a new store and office space. Unfortunately, this all occurred at about the time the Great Depression hit, and though the former post office building was demolished, no store was built on the site.

In March 1933, the Burger-Phillips mercantile finally moved from its original location to a new spot on Third Avenue, halfway between Nineteenth and Twentieth Streets. In November 1936, Burger-Phillips accomplished something of a first when it became the only store in Birmingham to have newfangled "magic doors" that automatically opened as customers approached, thanks to an electric eye device.

Burger-Phillips became the first of another breed, but the honor was dubious in this case. On June 10, 1975, the directors closed the downtown store and liquidated the assets, making it the first of the traditional, old-line downtown retailers to go out of business. Burger-Phillips might not have intended to start a trend, but over the next ten years, it would be joined by most of its retail brothers. For decades afterward, the rear brick wall of the vacant Burger-Phillips continued to bear a painted sign with the business's slogan: "Sooner or Later, Your Favorite Store."

Another of the downtown clothiers had an early history that was steeped in mystery, seemingly even to the store itself. Taking its cue from Paris, France's reputation as the fashion standard, at some point, a store known as "the Parisian" set up shop in Birmingham. But just when did this take place? In 1971, when the city was observing its centennial, even the store's officials had to admit they did not know. The statement they issued at that time read:

> *Parisian's research team can trace the store's history back to an ad which ran on April 6, 1889. We were then located at 2030 First Avenue North, Birmingham's main street, and were apparently well established. Then, as now, we were a fashion specialty store, and the advertisement featured ladies' dresses and hats, novelties and furnishings. Dresses and hats of superior quality could be made on short order.*
>
> *Beyond 1889, our research fades into the twilight zone. In the early 1930s, old-time employees were saying the store's founding was in the 1870s, but we have no way of proving it.*

Later, someone determined that the original founders were two sisters, Bertha and Estalla Sommers, and that they opened their Parisian Dry Goods and Millinery Company in October 1887. In 1911, ownership was transferred to Louis Gelders and G.W. Beringer, and it was then purchased by Laurens Bloch in 1918.

All of this ended up having little bearing on the future, as the Parisian story really gets underway in 1920, when it was purchased from Bloch by Carl Hess and his partner, William Holiner. A close look at any Parisian ads from the 1920s will show the "Holiner and Hess" credit along with the Parisian logo. During all this time, Parisian apparently migrated from one site to another, spending a while on the south side of Third Avenue between Nineteenth and Twentieth Streets, and by 1928, occupying space on the north side of Third Avenue across from the newly opened Alabama Theatre.

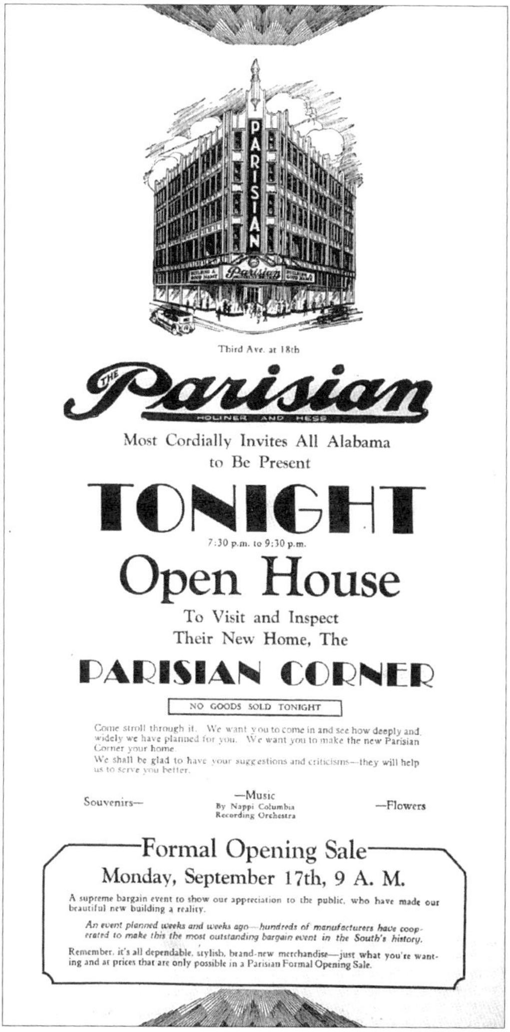

The Parisian, as it was originally known, decided to join big boys Loveman's and Pizitz when, in September 1928, it opened this multistory facility at the corner of Third Avenue and Eighteenth Street.

It was at that point that Holiner and Hess decided to install their Parisian store in a magnificent edifice that would put it in the same league as Pizitz and Loveman's. They built their striking five-story monument to retail success at the corner of Third Avenue and Eighteenth Street, across the street from the Lyric Theatre.

The store had its official open house on September 15, 1928. Whereas up to that point—as it would be later—Parisian was known primarily as a clothing store, there is no doubt that Holiner and Hess intended for their new building to be a true department store of the Pizitz and Loveman's persuasion. Newspaper coverage of the grand opening listed the departments that had been newly added, including a pharmacy, jewelry department, an on-site optometrist and those true department store staples: a soda fountain and lunch counter. There was even a candy department, with goodies that were made and packaged within the store. Staying true to its name, the new Parisian made much of its "French Room" on the third floor, "where are kept the higher priced hats." Such features as this would soon prove to be a liability rather than an asset, through no fault of Parisian's.

When the Depression made its unwanted appearance in October 1929, barely over a year after the huge new Parisian opened, luxury items immediately became the first casualties. People still had to have clothes, of course, but not the type Parisian was selling. The corporation had to be reorganized, but after some complicated financial maneuvering, Holiner and Hess managed to regain control of Parisian. In late August 1933, they closed the enormous store on a Monday and reopened in a new location on Thursday.

The former Parisian building sat vacant for a few months before becoming the temporary home of Loveman's after the disastrous March 1934 fire. Loveman's occupied the building until November 1935, and in 1940, it became the home of Calder Furniture for the next dozen years. By the late 1950s, all five floors were occupied by various U.S. Army offices. In the early 1960s, the ground floor served as a number of different discount department store chains, including Gulf Mills and John's Bargain Stores. In 1968, A.G. Gaston purchased the building for his Citizens Federal Bank operation. At that point, it received a "modernizing" facelift, which replaced the original terra cotta with concrete slabs and removed the towering pylon that had served as space for its identifying signage. Only the building's basic silhouette remained unchanged.

Meanwhile, the "new" new Parisian was on Second Avenue, in the building formerly known as the Caheen Brothers store. This slimmed-down Parisian had three floors of merchandise as of its opening, but in 1939, it expanded to include the top two floors of the building next door as well. Like most of the other stores, it underwent several facelifts over the course of its career, the most memorable of which took place in 1950. This one gave the front of the building the streamlined look most people remember, with the name spelled out in glowing blue lettering.

By 1989, most of the other department stores had abandoned downtown, and Parisian squatted on the nearly empty Second Avenue like a lone

After the Great Depression forced Parisian to move to smaller quarters on Second Avenue, the store underwent several remodelings to remain up to date. This is the look most people remember, with Parisian's gleaming white front and the name spelled out in glowing blue lettering.

Frenchman. However, instead of leaving the area completely, Parisian did an unusual thing for its time. The brand-new thirty-two-story Regions Harbert Plaza office building was being built at Sixth Avenue North and Twentieth Street, near Linn Park and City Hall, and Parisian simply packed up its clothing and trekked up to a space on the ground floor of the new location.

In the 1990s, Parisian was the only one of the locally owned department stores of old to still have a downtown presence. Even at that, though, things were much different than when it was comfortably situated in its earlier locations. For business, it depended totally on the office workers of its neighborhood, not shoppers out for a weekend spree downtown. In fact, the store was not even open on weekends, and operated only while city offices and the surrounding banking and legal district was open.

The beginning of Parisian's finis came in 1996, when Emil Hess, son of Carl Hess, died at age seventy-eight. Although he could not claim his father had been the founder of the store, the Hess family had been a part of its operation for so long that he may as well have been. The final blow came in August 2006, when North Carolina's Belk Inc. bought Parisian, with the understanding that only one of them would be the surviving name, and it would not be Parisian. A year later, Belk signs replaced the Parisian signs and, as a *Birmingham News* writer phrased it, "erased the historic Parisian name from department store retailing." Belk seemed to have little interest in preserving Parisian's commitment to its native downtown either and, after operating the Regions Harbert Plaza store under the Belk banner for a short while, closed it in January 2009.

Another pioneering name on the downtown clothing racks began in 1900 as Volley, Bowman and Bowers. Now, listen closely, because its names rotated quite a bit during the next few years. In 1903, apparently Volley and Bowman were out, and it became Cotten, Odum and Bowers. In 1915, Cotten was sacked, and the name became Odum, Bowers and White, which it would remain for the next sixty-three years.

Thankfully, even after W.W. Odum left the business to open his own Odum Clothing Company on Twentieth Street, the company elected not to change the name of the store again. Its biggest challenge was a fire in 1939 that completely destroyed the building, which was promptly reconstructed. At the time of the fire, store president Harry L. White issued a statement to the firm's loyal customers:

> *No expense will be spared to give you the type of store which you anticipate. All of the fine lines of merchandise with which the name of Odum, Bowers and White has been inseparably connected in the past will then once more be found here in the new store…every item reflecting style and attractiveness and meeting a continuance of your insistence that Odum, Bowers and White shall be in the vanguard with all that is new and fine and worthwhile in things to wear for men and women.*

(It is difficult to imagine the manager of a present-day Walmart issuing an edict in such high-flying language.)

The 1939 store might have been dripping with class and culture, but in 1948, it was again remodeled, adding the pink marble front that survives today. Like most of the others, Odum, Bowers and White could not survive the changing face of downtown, and it closed in September 1978.

With all the venerable old establishments making a big deal about how long they had been in business to serve the community, it seemed somewhat odd that two of the clothing stores survived for decades with the word "new" in their names. The New Ideal and New Williams maintained those names even after they had gotten to be as old as their neighbors, probably leading some people—especially recent Birmingham arrivals, who would not have been accustomed to them—to wonder where the names came from. That question is a little difficult to answer, but I'll try to do it in a shorthand manner.

It seems that in 1918, Joe Goldstein opened a store in a building that had formerly been known as the S.A. Williams store. For reasons now lost to the ages, rather than changing the name, Goldstein began calling his store New Williams, and the name held on. In later years, various branches of the Goldstein family would go on to lend their names and expertise to other Birmingham retail establishments, including Golbro (an abbreviation for Goldstein Bros.) and the giant discount department store G*E*S.

Perhaps the name New Williams was more appropriate than anyone thought, because a series of mishaps caused it to be made over more often than just about any other store downtown. A fire in early 1943 did some damage, and a major modernization project was barely finished in 1958 when a second fire swept through the building. Another fire in February 1980 caused the store to be closed for seven months while repairs were made. The Goldsteins were happy to give credit to the fire department for helping extinguish the blaze; the quick-thinking firefighters threw tarps over the merchandise to prevent any more water damage than absolutely necessary.

Herman Goldstein was president of New Williams when, in January 1983, he announced the store was closing. "I believe downtown has some problems," he understated, "and it'll take a lot of effort to get it back anywhere near what it was. I don't think it'll happen in the next three, four or five years."

Another large retailing family, the Alands, had begun operating the Ideal Cloak and Millinery Company in 1908. When Louis Saks vacated his store on the northeast corner of First Avenue and Nineteenth Street in 1916 (more about Louis and his store in the next chapter), Ideal moved into his former space. Around 1928, a lavish six-story structure was built adjoining the former Saks site. By the late 1930s, the store had moved to the middle of the south side of Second Avenue and changed its name to the New Ideal to celebrate the relocation. Finally, in January 1942, it moved into its permanent home, the building at the corner of Second Avenue and Eighteenth Street that had been vacated by Sears the previous fall (a story that is also coming up in the next chapter).

The New Ideal, even in its old age, sold a wide variety of women's, men's and children's clothing, but it became particularly famous as a source for wedding and prom dresses. Former customers readily admit, however, that

The Aland family opened the Ideal department store on Nineteenth Street around 1928. By the time of this early 1930s photo, the store had expanded all the way to the corner of First Avenue North. Also visible in the distance is a now forgotten retailer that was part of a chain known as the L.F.M. Stores, and across the street is the original Britling Cafeteria.

it was not uncommon to buy such special outfits at New Ideal but keep their origins secret, leaving others to speculate that they came from one of the more "upscale" stores. By catering to the common horde, New Ideal managed to stay in business into the 1990s, when many others had already locked their doors for the final time.

Although Yeilding's became known as primarily a clothing store, it actually began in 1876 as a farm supply store in the building that would later become the Bencor Hotel and eventually Blach's. Legend says the increasing downtown traffic frightened the horses belonging to the farmers, who came in their buggies and wagons to shop at the store, so in 1911, Yeilding's was forced to move out to what was then the boondocks, the corner of Second Avenue and Twenty-Second Street, far away from the downtown madness. The preponderance of two's in its address at least made the new location easy to memorize.

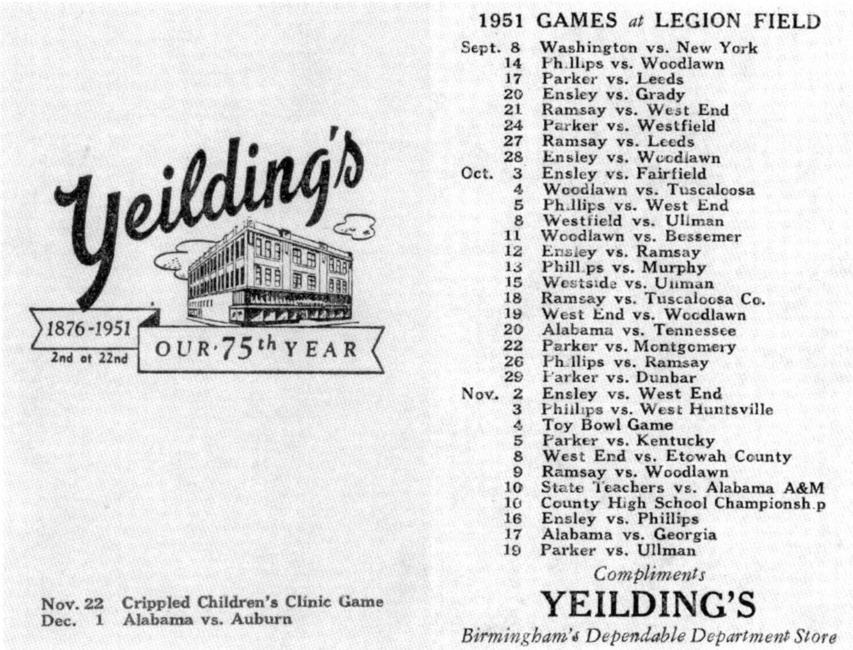

Yeilding's began as a farm supply store but was later known for selling clothing exclusively. In this promotional card from 1951, Yeilding's promoted its seventy-fifth anniversary as well as that autumn's schedule of football games at legendary Legion Field.

As the years poked by like an old plowhorse, Yeilding's slowly evolved from a farm supply/general merchandise store. As late as 1948, Yeilding's (sometimes still referred to by its official name, Yeilding Brothers) still had grocery and farm equipment departments, relics of its beginnings. A major remodeling program in 1955 turned the third floor into a "home floor," selling appliances, furniture, paint and other such necessities. The company never failed to point out, quite rightfully, that it was Birmingham's oldest department store.

That designation was gradually altered into "Birmingham's oldest retail outlet" because throughout the 1960s and 1970s, Yeilding's continued to evolve into a specialist in clothing, eventually women's clothing exclusively. In March 1981, Yeilding's closed the traditional old downtown store in favor of opening an Eastwood Mall location. The building was immediately occupied by Calder Furniture, whose former location on Second Avenue was destroyed by fire in October 1980. Besides the new Eastwood Mall store, Yeilding's had branches at Vestavia, Five Points West, Gardendale and Huntsville.

During the last weekend of 1996, the Yeilding's chain itself went out of business. The day of the family-run clothing store was long past; company president Richard Yeilding said a lot in a few words: "In the past year we've been downsizing, cutting back to make it work. But in retail business, trying to make it smaller after it's been big *never* works."

All the family businesses discussed had long and glorious histories, but even the most bewhiskered of them looked like a toddler when compared to Birmingham's downtown jewelry institution, Bromberg and Co. It is believed that Bromberg's is the oldest retail establishment in the state, having been started by Frederick Bromberg in Mobile in 1836.

The founder's grandson was responsible for the move to Birmingham in 1900, and for almost a half century, Bromberg's shifted from one location to another, starting on First Avenue North and then spending the bulk of the time on Twentieth Street. In 1943, a prime piece of downtown real estate suddenly became available when the long-established Drennen Store burned to the ground. Its position on the southeastern corner of Second Avenue and Twentieth Street was too valuable to sit empty, and Bromberg's promptly made arrangements to build a new store there as soon as the wartime restrictions on materials ended.

The new Bromberg's showplace opened in July 1946. Like the company it housed, the building came with a prestigious pedigree, designed by J. Gordon Carr, the same architect responsible for Tiffany's Fifth Avenue store in New York City. At the time, it was promoted as the "first example of pure contemporary architecture in the city," and much attention was given to its most noticeable feature: the "Shafts of Light," two windows that extended nearly the entire height of the building.

Although rightfully known as a jeweler, Bromberg's had many other features that were transferred to the new store from its previous locations. The company had become the first Eastman Kodak franchisee in Alabama, and thus its photography department and film processing service were legendary. A focal point of the new store was a huge grandfather clock that had been in the family since the real grandfather had purchased it en route to America in 1835. The third floor even served as an antique store of sorts, where "centuries-old silver, exquisite pieces of Sevres, Lowestoff, Worcester, Staffordshire, Crow Darby and other collector's delights in china" could be purchased. Along with the nearby Melba Theater, opened that same year, the new Bromberg's was a sure sign that the restrictions of the austere World War II years were over.

Before and after its much-heralded new building, Bromberg's held its own in the changing downtown scene through the Depression, two world wars,

As soon as World War II was over, upscale Bromberg's Jewelers wasted no time in constructing an impressive new flagship store on the corner of Second Avenue and Twentieth Street. By having all plans and materials prepared in anticipation of the war's end, the new home of Bromberg's was able to open in the summer of 1946.

civil unrest and goodness knows what other obstacles. However, there came a challenge it could not overcome, although not for lack of trying.

In 2001, Frank Bromberg Jr. (great-grandson of the company founder) had told newspapers, "Downtown will never be what it was 40 years ago, but it's been good to us. Every company needs a landmark location. Why not downtown?" Why not, indeed? The Brombergs had every intention of maintaining the status quo, but then came the recession that began in 2008. Frank Bromberg III echoed his father when he said, "Obviously, shopping downtown is not what it used to be, and this didn't happen overnight. It makes sense in the current economic environment to move merchandise to stores where it has a better chance of selling." The downtown Bromberg's store closed on March 6, 2009.

Unlike so many of the other former downtown retailers, the Brombergs did not walk away from their prized building. Even though its merchandise was distributed among its branch stores in Mountain Brook, the Riverchase Galleria and the Summit, Bromberg's offices and a variety of other services remained in the downtown flagship structure. Not wanting it to look like an abandoned site, the Brombergs continued to use the large display windows for merchandise that was available at their other locations. And with an eye toward better times in the future and the growing number of people choosing to live downtown, the family announced that there would still be the possibility of reopening the store for retail purposes. That, by itself, was far different from anything else that had been said on the closing of the other downtown giants.

Chapter 3
LINKS IN THE CHAINS

There is a lot to be said for, and learned from, the many downtown stores that were founded and nurtured by local businesspeople. However, there were others that became a vital part of the Birmingham scene even though they were outlets of national corporations with branches all over the United States. It is to those stores of nonlocal origin that we now turn our attention.

First, however, it should be mentioned that not all the national chains that attempted to get a toehold in Birmingham did so successfully. Take the case of Chicago-based Montgomery Ward, for example. The mail order catalog monarch opened a store in Birmingham somewhere around 1927 and, for a few years, did a pretty good business on First Avenue. Despite a remodeling program in 1930, economic conditions no doubt hastened Montgomery Ward's departure, never to return to the city. (If the store had stuck around until 1939, Birmingham shoppers could have been among the first to receive copies of Montgomery Ward's new Christmas book featuring the company's own creation, Rudolph the Red-Nosed Reindeer.)

A similar situation took place in the vastly different world of the mid-1950s, when the Belk-Hudson chain set up an outlet on Second Avenue, near the Comer Building. By the time the Birmingham branch opened, Belk-Hudson was operating 335 outlets in the South, but after a short stay, the Birmingham Belk-Hudson was sent packing, reducing that number to 334. Of course, as we saw in the last chapter, Belk was not gone for good. In 2006, it would return hungrily, with a craving for French food, and would devour Parisian without even leaving any bones to spit out.

In contrast to the brief Birmingham careers of Montgomery Ward and Belk-Hudson, the gritty survivor of the downtown chain stores was J.J. Newberry. As a national chain, the store's history dated back to 1911, when John J. Newberry started his "dime stores" (a name later changed to "variety stores" after inflation hit) in the New York area. In Birmingham, its early history was intertwined with that of the building, which came with a rich pedigree of its own.

The corner that was later home to Newberry's was originally the site of the Florence Hotel. Those accommodations were vacated in 1916, when Louis Saks decided to move his business a block north of its original location at First Avenue and Nineteenth Street. The new Saks building was truly impressive, with six floors plus a basement. A huge Saks sign was prominently mounted on the roof, leading those who have seen it in vintage photos to surmise the building was a branch of New York's famed Saks Fifth Avenue. (Considering that one Herman Saks was operating a store at the other end of the block, that was obviously a very good last name to have in the store industry.)

It must be that Louis Saks's business, like so many others, was unable to survive the Depression because by the early 1930s a new owner had come to town. Clem Melançon (his name pronounced MEL-an-son) had been operating stores on the East Coast since 1908, but in 1933, he elected to cast his lot with Birmingham. In the autumn of that year, Melançon put up his logo, described by the newspaper as a "great green star," on the former Saks store, using the same framework that had formerly supported the Saks sign. At the time Melançon moved in, the building was already partly leased by a much smaller version of J.J. Newberry, and the two disparate stores managed to coexist under the same roof for the next three years.

In August 1936, Melançon issued a statement in his newspaper ads that explained why he was abruptly pulling up stakes:

> *Saying good-bye to Birmingham and Alabama is indeed a hard thing to do, for this city and state have been very kind to me and my entire organization since my opening just three years ago. As the newspapers stated, I had a lease for ten more years, proving that I had intended to make this city my future home. But the Newberry offer for the remaining ten years was so flattering, I was advised to accept it by the many civic leaders I consulted.*

We can only guess what sort of offer he couldn't refuse had been made to Melançon by the owners of Newberry's, but the result was that Melançon relinquished control of the entire building to J.J. Newberry, took his profits and left town. A few people continued to remember his role in downtown retailing, and when he died at his home in Daytona Beach, Florida, in 1966, his passing was briefly noted in the Birmingham papers.

Meanwhile, Newberry's spread out over its new domicile and truly made the space its own. A major revitalization project was undertaken in May 1961 that would transform the former variety store into something much bigger—literally, as the remodeling added twenty-five thousand square feet of retail space to the existing space and turned Newberry's into a true department store, not a typical five-and-dime.

Apparently, after J.J. Newberry moved into what had originally been built as Louis Saks's department store in 1916, at least one vestige of previous tenant Melancon's remained, in the form of the giant green star crowning the roofline.

At the same time the interior was remodeled, there was some even more noticeable work on the outside. The sides of the building received new aluminum panels bearing Newberry's trademark color of aquamarine. A tall aquamarine panel extended the entire height of the building on its corner, with Newberry spelled out in huge vertical letters. But when it came to the signage at street level, a bit of a split personality seemed to creep in. On the Nineteenth Street side, the sign gave the full name, J.J. Newberry Co. However, on the Second Avenue side, the sign read simply "Newberry." Most of the public ignored both names and simply called the store Newberry's.

In December 1962, there was an odd veering off the track, especially considering all the work that had been done just a year and a half earlier.

Everything remained basically the same, but the Newberry signs came down, to be replaced by a new logo, Britt's. The relationship between the two was never spelled out explicitly, but it was worth noting that the same store executives from New York presided at both the opening of the remodeled Newberry's and the opening of Britt's. The two were apparently branches of the same company, and while Britt's tried to make a non-Newberry's name for itself downtown, the Newberry's at Eastwood Mall continued on its merry way. (As we shall see in our final chapter, this brief interlude ensured that when the landmark civil rights protests of 1963 came about, it was Britt's lunch counter, and not Newberry's, that made the news.)

When Newberry's abruptly returned in May 1965, it was as if Britt's had never been there. At least now the store's name became more standardized, with both sides of the building sporting the new, more modern Newberry's logo with an enlarged initial *N*. For the next three decades, Newberry's was a Second Avenue fixture, never flashy or attracting attention like Pizitz or

In the early 1960s, Newberry's received a facelift that included the aquamarine aluminum siding that was the chain's trademark color. This aerial view captures the proximity of Newberry's to its fellow Second Avenue variety stores H.L. Green and W.T. Grant. *Birmingham, Alabama Public Library Archives, Catalogue #854.828.1A.*

Loveman's, but a reliable presence for those needing variety store goods or a quick lunch counter snack.

By the 1990s, J.J. Newberry Co. was only one division of another long-established variety store conglomerate, the McCrory Corporation. Other formerly independent chains that were now part of the McCrory empire included G.C. Murphy and TG&Y. McCrory/Newberry's lease in Birmingham entitled it to its space through 1994. It made it, but just barely.

With all the surrounding stores having closed long ago (with the only possible exception, Parisian, moving uptown), Newberry's shut down in January 1995, but not for lack of business. The city had decided it wanted that spot to build the new IMAX theater adjacent to the McWane Science Center being installed in the former Loveman's building, and Newberry's was in the way. Therefore, over the customers' objections, the city bought the property and evicted its tenant. It was a somewhat ignominious ending for such a veteran store, but when the newspapers quoted the manager as saying Newberry's was founded in 1916 by the Newberry family of Birmingham, it looked like no one really knew the story behind the store anyway. He obviously confused the store's age with the year Louis Saks's building was constructed, but it is harder to explain how he was seemingly unaware that "his" Newberry's was only one outpost in a national chain.

Some of the building's exterior ornamentation was preserved and sits quietly today in storage in the McWane Science Center next door. The aquamarine metal siding, however, went down with the ship—er, store. Even if not for the city's desire to use that particular corner, Newberry's time was almost up anyway. In February 2002, the McCrory Corporation ceased all operations, shutting down its remaining outlets of its various chains, so at least the Newberry's building in Birmingham never had to sit abandoned and become an eyesore.

While Newberry's was a Yankee chain that invaded the beloved Southland, the S.H. Kress stores actually began in the South. Samuel H. Kress himself was a native of Pennsylvania, but seeing the need for more retail outlets in the smaller southern cities and towns, he opened his first five-and-ten store in Memphis in 1896. Naturally, it did not take long for him to branch into Birmingham.

There are vague historical references to the first Kress in Birmingham opening in 1899. Indications are that it was on Third Avenue, in the building that later became Odum, Bowers and White. In 1915, Kress built what would be its most notable early Birmingham location, smack in the middle of Second Avenue between Nineteenth and Twentieth Streets, and sporting

In September 1937, S.H. Kress moved from its 1915 building on Second Avenue to this impressive edifice at the corner of Third Avenue and Nineteenth Street. The structure was purposely designed to resemble a scaled-down version of Kress's flagship store on New York City's Fifth Avenue.

an ornamental terra-cotta façade that, by that time, was a trademark of the Kress locations.

(As an aside, one can be forgiven for confusing the S.H. Kress stores with another dime store chain, S.S. Kresge. In fact, at one point, the two variety store founders made an agreement that neither would open a store in the same area where the other was already operating, as severe bafflement from their target shoppers would be inevitable. That agreement did not stand forever—Kresge had a Birmingham store at Eastwood Mall by the early 1960s—but in the end, the Kresge name was almost forgotten when the company switched over to its larger discount department store chain, Kmart.)

By the late 1930s, Kress had outgrown the Second Avenue facility and decided that if it were going to build again, this time it would build big. At the corner of Third Avenue and Nineteenth Street, the former Blach's store was leveled, and in its place arose a Kress that was intended to replicate the chain's Fifth Avenue, New York location. Opening in September 1937, the new Kress was by far the most lavish five-and-ten Birmingham had ever seen. One of the building's most striking architectural features was its flagpole support, with huge K-R-E-S-S letters in glowing red neon. Many years later, store manager Bruce Braswell reminisced in a letter:

> *These stores were very large for those days, having terrazzo floors in the sales areas, high ceilings with huge chandeliers and indirect lighting, large mirrored columns throughout sales floors, and wide sections in walls around the sales floors, colorfully decorated with merchandise. Shiny brass rails lined the stairways down to the lower sales floor. A very large luncheonette was located at one end of the lower floor and had a bustling noontime business from nearby office workers and shoppers. The second floor was for the office, receiving room and layaway storage. The third and fourth floors were reserve stock rooms. Large display show windows were on the two sides facing the sidewalks and streets, as was customary in stores then.*

The Kress legacy in Birmingham amounted to more than just cheap knickknacks. Samuel Kress amassed an enormous and expensive collection of fine art from the sales of his nickel-and-dime merchandise, and he shared his wealth by dividing up his priceless pieces among various art museums in the cities where his stores had been most successful. The Kress Collection is today still a significant part of the Birmingham Museum of Art.

Regardless of Kress's philanthropic leanings, or the civil rights sit-ins that took place at its lunch counter, when the announcement was made that the

The pioneer of all the national variety store chains was F.W. Woolworth. This was most likely its earliest outlet in Birmingham, in the former location of the Ferd Marx Store. Next-door neighbor Caheen Brothers would be replaced by Parisian in 1933; amazingly, both store buildings still exist, but they have been remodeled beyond all recognition.

downtown Kress would close its doors at the end of January 1978, it probably came as no surprise to anyone. As a store clerk said at the time, "I guess everybody lives out of town now, and they buy things near where they live. You just can't get people to come downtown and buy any more." Indeed, additional Kress locations in North Birmingham and Bessemer remained in business. But downtown, the huge, empty building was a sad sight with the Kress signs still in place on its sides and along the roofline and the no-longer-lighted neon letters on the base of the flagpole slowly rusting away.

As almost everyone knows, the true grandpappy of the five-and-ten world was Woolworth's. Even though as a national chain the F.W. Woolworth Co. dated back to 1876, there seems to be no definite historical record of when or where its first Birmingham outlet was established. By around 1910 or somewhere thereabouts, Woolworth's had moved into the Second Avenue building formerly occupied by the Ferd Marx store, and it remained there while its closest competitor, S.H. Kress, built its terra-cotta monument practically next door. At the time of the devastating Loveman's fire in 1934, Woolworth's was located across the street on the north side of Third Avenue, although just when that move had been made is not documented.

When Kress pulled out in front by erecting its huge Third Avenue store in 1937, it certainly lit a fire under Woolworth's as well. Within two years, Woolworth's had taken out a lease on three pieces of property on the corner facing the new Kress store and announced its intention to build its own flagship store that would be a duplicate of its New York location. (Like Kress, Woolworth had to scale things down for Birmingham, and its new building had only three stories instead of New York's five.) The former Woolworth building on Second Avenue would become a Walgreen drugstore in 1940 and, in the postwar world, was transformed beyond recognition into Mangel's department store.

Meanwhile, work got underway on the corner location. As with Kress, a small percentage of the building was actually used for selling merchandise. The basement contained housewares and hardware, while the main floor displayed all the staples. The two upper floors were used for storage and other behind-the-scenes activities, such as "a room where girls do nothing but bag the candy you find so attractively packaged downstairs," as the newspapers droolingly phrased it.

Woolworth's whole idea was to beat Kress at its own Third Avenue game, and in the end, the five-and-dime patriarch got the last wheezy laugh. After the downtown Kress store closed in January 1978, Woolworth's managed to hold down its corner for just short of eleven more years, finally succumbing to the changing retail climate in December 1988. When the national Woolworth chain at last discontinued operations completely in 1997, everyone knew that it was indeed a different world than just a half century earlier.

Inspired by the S.H. Kress move, in 1939, Woolworth's also relocated to a prominent corner of Third Avenue and Nineteenth Street. Next door, the New Williams women's clothing store survived for decades with a sign bearing a misplaced apostrophe in "William's." *Birmingham, Alabama Public Library Archives, Catalogue #820.11.1.*

Kress and Woolworth had both started their national franchising in the late 1800s, but after the turn of the century, other would-be dime store despots began staking claims along America's main streets, not neglecting downtown Birmingham. Most, if not quite all, of them copied the S.H. Kress and F.W. Woolworth pattern of featuring the owner's first two initials combined with his last name. Falling right in line with this way of thinking was W.T. Grant, founded in 1906 and arriving in Birmingham in

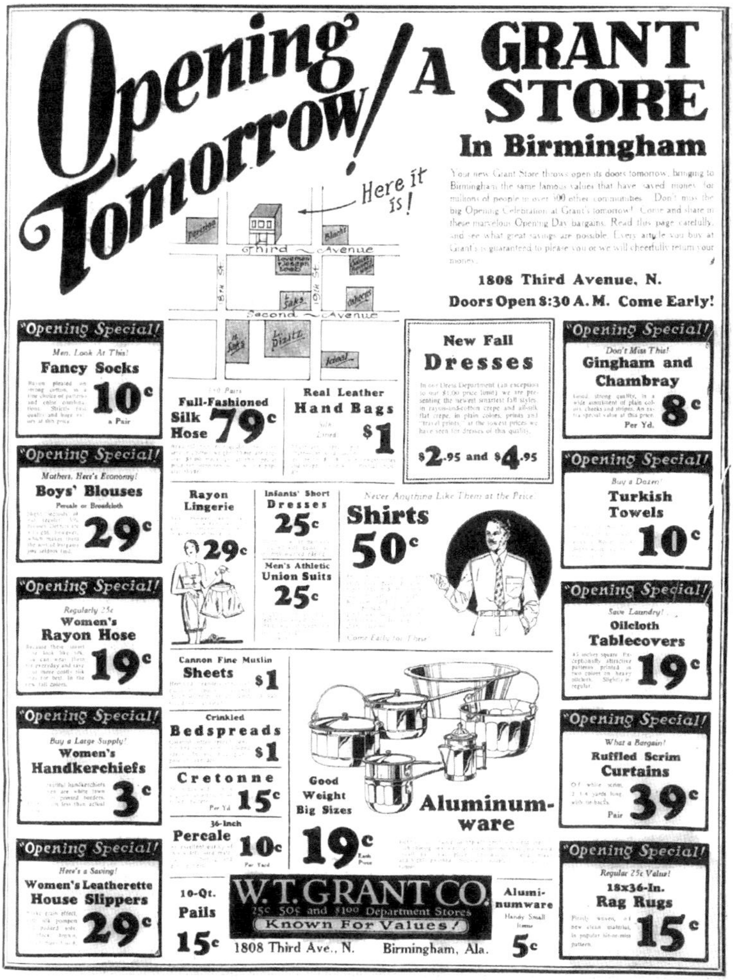

Another popular dime store chain was W.T. Grant. This September 1930 ad touts the company's arrival in Birmingham and helpfully illustrates the other major downtown stores in its neighborhood in an effort to help potential shoppers orient themselves to its location.

September 1930, initially in that same row of Third Avenue buildings as Woolworth's. When Kress moved to its spacious new structure in 1937, soon thereafter Grant's settled into the former Second Avenue Kress and remained there until early 1973. After attempting a Kmart-like transformation into a discount department store called Grant City (Birmingham had one on Green Springs Highway), the W.T. Grant chain closed all of its stores east of the Mississippi River in 1975.

Next door to Grant's was Silver's five-and-ten, which eventually became part of another initialed variety store chain, H.L. Green. There was little unique about this chain except the way it incorporated its name into some of the merchandise; a good example would be its private label "Green Kitten" ladies' hosiery, which came complete with artwork of an emerald-colored feline on the packaging.

Of course, in any discussion of chain outlets, we cannot forget the "world's largest store," as the initials of its Chicago radio station spelled out. There was a time, not that long ago, when retailing just did not come any bigger than Sears, Roebuck & Co.

Sears, as most people referred to it for convenience, began in 1886 as a strictly mail-order company, building its reputation on its ability to deliver anything from clothing to farm equipment to prefabricated houses to residents who lived too far out in the country to visit stores often. It was not until 1925 that the chain even considered the idea of opening its own retail stores, and even then, the early ones were not considered much more than adjuncts to the catalog business.

In fact, when Sears first came to Birmingham, this was still very much the line of thinking. Sears's two earliest Birmingham locations were not downtown, but on the south side of the city (one was across the street from the Hillman Hospital). It was not until around 1936 that Sears brought its "wish book" to life with a full-scale downtown store, located at the corner of Second Avenue and Eighteenth Street in the building that had previously been the Herman Saks store.

Proving that it liked to think big, no sooner had Sears moved into its new home than it began scouting locations for expansion. In 1937, the most likely spot appeared to be the former site of the demolished county courthouse at the corner of Third Avenue and Twenty-First Street. For reasons not made entirely clear, within two weeks of the announcement, there was an outcry from taxpayers accusing the city of playing dirty politics in order to gain Sears's favor. It all had to do with the lot in question being county property and Sears being a commercial entity and so on and so forth. Corruption in

The mammoth Sears, Roebuck & Co. built a sprawling one-story structure occupying most of two city blocks in 1941. In the summer of 1955, it received a major visual boost with the addition of this huge sign that spelled out the store's name in glowing green neon. *Dixie Neon collection.*

Jefferson County's politics was not new then and would eventually cease to be a novelty, but in 1937, the end result was that Sears dropped the idea. The property instead remained a parking lot until 2001, when today's Concord Center rose on the same spot.

After a few more years of snooping around, Sears found another prospective location, this time far out on the western edge of downtown's limits. But what a piece of property it was! Occupied by the Illinois Central Railroad at the time of purchase and formerly containing the city's streetcar barn, the lot encompassed two square city blocks between First and Second Avenues and Fourteenth and Sixteenth Streets. Sears crowed that when the facility was complete, it would be America's first large one-story department store. This was unheard of in the days when practically every department store towered three, four, five or six stories above the street. The new Sears would take all that retail space and spread it out over a single level.

The newfangled Sears opened on October 15, 1941. Much excitement surrounded the opening, but not nearly as much excitement as less than two months later, when Pearl Harbor was attacked on December 7. The war was especially hard on the new Sears, since it was located so far away from the rest of downtown. According to Birmingham historian and collector Alvin Hudson, the enormous Sears parking lot was virtually empty because gas and tire rationing had stopped people from driving. The lot was piled high with scrap metal gathered during the regular wartime drives to collect such material. (Well into the 1980s, that parking lot continued to betray its origins as the site of the streetcar barn, as abandoned and half-covered tracks crisscrossed the pavement without going anywhere in particular.)

When the war was finally over, everyone exhaled again, and the period of postwar prosperity and pure giddiness began. In its store newsletter, the Birmingham Sears got into the spirit of the times by poking fun at itself in a phony advertisement that would have made any professional satirist proud. Among the bogus merchandise was this one: "Yes sir, thousands of gallons of gasoline absolutely free! All you need is an Allsneak Siphon Tube, a dark street and a parked car…and don't forget the famous Allsneak Bail Bond Service." There was also "Genuine Missouri Mulehide Underwear," touted as giving "solid comfort, and we do mean solid. Guaranteed for 19 years, or longer if changed annually." And in women's clothing was the new rage, coats made from "Front Quarter Alabama Tomcat skins in two lovely hues—Mange Tan and Crummy Gray."

In the real world, the downtown Sears remained virtually unchanged from the day it opened, except for minor cosmetic improvements. In the 1950s, a huge green neon Sears sign was erected on the First Avenue corner of the building, visible for blocks around. In the 1960s, Sears made a honey of a deal with the Walt Disney Studios to be the purveyors of a line of Winnie-the-Pooh clothing and toys, and soon, the children's department of the downtown store was transformed into an outpost of the Hundred-Acre Wood. In early 1970, Sears added a Coffee House Restaurant so

Those who visited Sears in the 1960s still fondly remember the "Servaround," the round hot dog stand in the parking lot that was seemingly a necessary stop for hungry kids. *Polly Chambers collection.*

shoppers would not even have to leave the premises to fend off malnutrition. (Previously, hungry customers made do with a round hot dog stand, known as the Servaround, situated in the parking lot, and of course, there was always the Sears candy counter, with its roasted cashews and chocolate-covered raisins.)

All had seen better days by July 1990, when Sears closed the downtown store and ostensibly replaced it with a huge new facility on Weibel Drive in Fairfield. (The fact that the two locations were nowhere near each other seemed not to be a factor in this decision.) After closing, the old 1941 Sears building sat abandoned, attracting vagrants and graffiti. For years, a powder blue curtain that made up part of the décor in the women's clothing department could still be seen in a corner window, hanging in tatters. Finally, all the door and window openings were sealed off with cement blocks, turning the decaying old building into the tomb it appeared to be—part of the charm of downtown that was buried inside.

Chapter 4

THE REST AND THE RESTAURANTS

Of course, downtown's distinct character was made up of many different things, somewhat like a giant patchwork quilt that one could walk around inside. All of the large stores mentioned up to this point were vastly important, but there were scores of smaller businesses filling in the gaps and contributing much to the overall hustle and bustle that characterized the city streets.

We have already mentioned Calder Furniture, which spent a dozen years in the ill-fated Parisian building, many more next door to Newberry's and ended up in the former Yeilding's building. Plenty of other furniture stores hung their drawers downtown, including Rhodes-Carroll, R.B. Broyles and Haverty Furniture. For those with a taste for musical furniture, there was E.E. Forbes Piano Co. on Fourth Avenue and its rival, Phipps Pianos, on Third Avenue. ("Walk a block and save!" Phipps's TV commercials barked.) There was also Harry Charles's piano store, with the unforgettable slogan, "To pay more is sheer extravagance."

There were other department stores that operated on a much more modest scale than their gargantuan rivals. Ferd Weil and his partner, Paul Vaughan, opened their Vaughan-Weil store in 1941. It had a prime location across the street from the Alabama Theatre, a block it shared with several other downtown fixtures. When Vaughan-Weil closed up in 1970, its women's fur business was doing so well that that single department simply moved down Third Avenue to the former Bond clothing store and operated as Weil Furs for many more years. (At least as of this writing, the rusted remnants of the Weil Furs neon sign can still be seen clinging to the building.) Tillman-Levenson was another partnership, beginning on First Avenue and then moving to the hinterlands beyond Sears in 1960. More than the rest, Tillman-Levenson was a discount store for Birmingham's huge population of laborers, specializing in economical work clothes, shoes and so on.

In 1948, Morris Sher opened a downtown shop he called the New York Clothing Company. According to family lore, Sher picked this name because he had gotten a good deal on a box of unclaimed stationery with a letterhead bearing that moniker, and rather than waste a bargain, he decided to use it for his Birmingham business on First Avenue. Few people even paid attention to the dislocated name because the store became better known for its slogan, "The Home of King Kredit."

Such a slogan called for a logo, and King Kredit (as the store quite naturally became known) used the visage of a grinning, bucktoothed, bald-headed ruler with small, square spectacles. The myopic monarch gazed down from the store's signage and also appeared as a mechanical figure

Discount clothier King Kredit had recently left its First Avenue location (in a portion of the former Ideal store) for the more bustling region of Third Avenue when this photo was taken; coincidentally, the neighbor it left behind, Lichter's (home of "Magic Credit"), would later move in next door to King Kredit's new location. *Dixie Neon collection.*

that sat in the forecourt, turning its head from side to side and frightening children and small animals.

King Kredit's kingdom later moved to a better-remembered location on Third Avenue but retained the hairless head as its logo; indoors, there was even a neon clock shaped like the potentate's pate. The secret to the store's immense success was spelled out by Morris Sher's sons:

> *Dad made a strategic decision that King Kredit was going to be the store with the easiest credit in town. Instead of having low prices and high credit standards, he figured if he got a down payment close to the cost of the merchandise, he could sell to everyone with little risk.*

Still later, the clothing store expanded to handle furniture and appliances, and by the time King Kredit grinned his last, the name had been changed to Mr. King Furniture. The jolly, but somewhat creepy, king continued to oversee the proceedings underneath him as long as the business lasted.

(Another furniture store nearby, Lichter's, also played up its "Magic Credit" to potential customers. Instead of a king, the Lichter's logo was a rabbit pulling a magician out of a hat; like King Kredit, the rabbit became an animated figure that performed in the store.)

Another business that became as famous for its storefront signage as anything else was Rosenberger's Birmingham Trunk, which began selling luggage in 1905. Within just a few years, Rosenberger's had picked up its trademark: a red elephant with one foot propped up on a trunk—the kind you pack things in, not the kind on the elephant's face. (This business name and logo were loaded with pachyderm-sized wordplay.) The elephant appeared in neon, projecting over Second Avenue near Pizitz, but its biggest claim in state history would occur almost an entire continent away.

In 1930, the University of Alabama football team journeyed to Pasadena to play in the Rose Bowl. As a gesture of pride, Rosenberger's supplied "good luck charms" bearing the elephant logo to the entire team. The legend goes that when the players arrived in California with red elephant emblems dangling from their luggage, the local sports writers made some sort of connection between that and the oversized football players, and suddenly the Crimson Tide had a crimson elephant as its logo. There are those who deny this account. But it's Rosenberger's story, and it's sticking with it.

One problem that never seemed to go away in the heart of downtown was parking. There were seemingly never enough spaces to allow everyone to conveniently visit their shopping or entertainment destinations, so during

According to tradition, the red elephant that was the trademark of Rosenberger's Birmingham Trunk was the inspiration for the elephant that still serves as the emblem of the University of Alabama football team. Whether one agrees with the story or not, the Rosenberger sign was an unforgettable sight on Second Avenue. *Dixie Neon collection.*

the 1950s, the city responded by putting up two small parking decks, where cars could be stacked into a pair of levels while reserving the ground level for still more retail space.

As the growing automobile culture created a parking problem downtown, one solution was to fill vacant corners with elevated parking decks. The decks on Fourth Avenue (top) and Second Avenue (bottom) reserved their ground floors for small retailers that included Krystal Hamburgers, Dixie Cream Donuts and Lorch's Jewelers.

One of these decks was on the northeast corner of Second Avenue and Eighteenth Street, where the old post office building had stood until the early 1930s. Some of the small businesses that occupied the street level of this deck have become the stuff of misty-eyed memories, including

One of the most legendary "under the parking deck" shops was Joe Rumore's Record Rack, owned by the popular WVOK radio personality. Here, crowds are packing the store's small space to meet an up-and-coming comedian named Andy Griffith, signing his hit record "What It Was, Was Football." *Rumore Family collection.*

the Krystal Hamburgers stand on the corner, a magic shop, Dixie Cream Donuts and, most famous of all, Joe Rumore's Record Rack, a tiny space operated by one of the most famous radio personalities in town. This deck and its attendant businesses were demolished to make way for another parking deck, this time the one built by Loveman's in 1971 and still used by the McWane Science Center.

The other deck was on the southeast corner of Fourth Avenue and Nineteenth Street and sat where the Birmingham City Hall had stood until being removed to Woodrow Wilson Park in 1950. The deck took the aging and often fire-damaged structure's place shortly thereafter. Its stores were not quite as high profile as those of the Second Avenue deck, but most people would remember Lorch's Jewelers on the corner and a huge neon Coca-Cola billboard (complete with a clock) perched above. Peering closely at vintage photos, it is amusing to note that several ground-level businesses continued to use "City Hall" as part of their names long after that municipal building had moved north. Even though this deck still stands, today, the ground-floor location of all those former businesses has, as one might expect, been converted into more parking spaces.

Now, in order for shoppers to manage to get around to all these various stores and shops, they had to have sustenance. Other than the aforementioned Krystal and Dixie Cream Donuts, fast food restaurants could not be found just everywhere; in fact, until the 1950s, they hardly existed at all, so it was up to the downtown restaurants to dish up dishes for those who needed a bit of strengthening before continuing their shopping expeditions.

Probably no single downtown restaurant was as beloved as Joy Young. During its sixty-year sojourn, the name of the place probably made most people wonder who this mysterious Mr. Young was, as he never seemed to be on the premises. In fact, there was no Mr. Young. Joy Young was founded by four partners who had made their way to Birmingham from their homeland in Canton, China: Mansion Joe, Loo Choy, Loo Bing and George Sai. The restaurant they opened in 1920 was given the name "King Joy" and operated out of a portion of the Burger-Phillips department store while it was still in its Second Avenue digs. Business was brisk, no doubt owing to the novelty of a Chinese restaurant when there were few people of that nationality in Birmingham. Rumor has it that in the early days, Joy Young received an unwelcome visit from the Ku Klux Klan, which expressed strong feelings about its non–North American ownership. But the regular customer base stood up for those egg rolls, and the publicity only increased business substantially.

Seeking larger quarters, in 1925, the business changed its name to Joy Young and moved to its longstanding location on Twentieth Street, between Fourth and Fifth Avenues. This put it in proximity to Birmingham's "hotel row," the string of rooming establishments that clustered near the opulent railroad terminal. With its flashy neon signage reminiscent of the city's glamorous movie theaters, Joy Young was a sight to behold, day or night.

Those who did not wish to be beheld could take advantage of Joy Young's famed private booths, where guests could nibble at their food (or each other) behind thin drapes. Even though Chinese food was the whole reason for Joy Young's existence, it also became known for its southern fried chicken, and Henry Joe, grandson of the founder, says that their chicken outsold the more ethnic dishes by a large margin. Those who were in the mood to try something a bit more exotic usually gravitated toward the aforementioned egg rolls, which the cooks would begin making at 4:00 a.m. (Fortunately, the cooks all lived in apartments on the second floor of the building, so they didn't have far to travel to get to work at that time of day.)

With all the hotels and department stores that supplied Joy Young's customers slowly fading into the pavement, it was not surprising when the

Few restaurants in downtown Birmingham were as beloved as Joy Young, which built its reputation on Chinese food but also did a finger-lickin' good business with its southern fried chicken. This September 1954 ad appeared after the famous eatery had been closed for a remodeling program.

Joe family announced that they would abandon their downtown location for the more profitable suburbs around Brookwood Village Mall in September 1980. The closing was the subject of much media attention, but in the end, many customers simply followed the trail of egg rolls to Brookwood and continued their patronage. Even the heavy glass panels with their rampant red-and-green dragons were transported from downtown to the new location, just to give some continuity. After changing locations another time or two, Joy Young ended its career in Pelham in the mid-1990s as a carry-out counter only, still specializing in those famous egg rolls.

Whereas there was only one Joy Young—or at least, only one at any given time—there was another name in eating that was scattered all over downtown and eventually throughout Jefferson County. No matter which street or avenue you happened to find yourself strolling down, you could not avoid passing a Britling Cafeteria before too long. Now, we have already learned that there was no such person named Joy Young, but surely the Britling restaurants were started by a Mr. Britling, weren't they? Wrong again!

The first Britling was opened in 1919 by A.W.B. Johnson and was reportedly the first cafeteria in the entire South. So why wasn't it called Johnson's? No, it was not because of possible confusion with Howard Johnson's, which had not yet been founded. It seems that Johnson (A.W.B., not Howard) was an H.G. Wells fan, and he named his new restaurant after one of that author's books, *Mr. Britling Sees It Through*. The cafeteria concept certainly saw it through, becoming more popular in the South than in any other part of the country. Historians have attributed this success to the fact that cafeterias bridged the gap between the two most extreme classes of eateries: the food was inexpensive and plentiful, but the facilities were considerably more elegant than the typical southern roadhouse.

Within a few years of its opening, Britling had been acquired by the Holcomb family, who would hold onto it for the next fifty years and truly make it their own (the name notwithstanding). By that time, there were three Britlings in the chain: the original on First Avenue, one on Third Avenue and one on Twentieth Street. Actually, the latter two were a single entity but operated separately. The kitchen area was shared by both, but diners could enter from only one side or the other.

A 1927 article on the chain's phenomenal popularity gives some insight into the different era in which it was written, both in its language and description of customs:

Britling Cafeterias had locations throughout downtown Birmingham and, later, in the suburbs. This was the storefront on busy Twentieth Street; although there was another entrance just around the corner on Third Avenue, the two were considered separate businesses, and there was no access from one side to the other.

Would you think that the Britlings have their good days—that is, regular good days? Well, they do and they are Mondays, Thursdays and Saturdays. Why? Mondays bring to town the housewives seeking bargains from the

> *retail merchants. Thursdays bring cook's night off and so has become in many Birmingham homes "Britling Night." Saturday is half holiday for many employees and they like to take plenty of time for luncheon, and then there are the matinees.*

The same article reported that Britling had become very popular with small children, a fact that was apparently as true in the 1960s as it was in the 1920s. Britling became one of the longtime sponsors of Birmingham's *Romper Room* franchise on WAPI-TV. When children ate at a Britling location, they would be given a specially marked card if they drank all their milk. When the designated card was completed, they would receive a ceramic mug with the Britling logo on one side and the grinning *Romper Room* jack-in-the-box on the other.

In this view of Twenty-First Street at Second Avenue, we can see Joe's Steak House Restaurant, and if one squints very hard, in the distance is the original location of John's Restaurant, which now operates only a few doors south of where Joe's appears here. *Dixie Neon collection.*

By the time of its television sponsorship days, Britling had long since expanded from downtown into the suburbs. The original First Avenue location had closed in 1964, when the building in which it was located was sold, but the others held on. In 1972, even a new downtown location was opened, in the recently constructed First National–Southern Natural building. Branches could be found at Western Hills Mall, Five Points West, Parkway East, Highland Avenue, Mountain Brook, Vestavia, Hoover and Huntsville.

Not all the Britling locations closed down at the same time, although the two remaining original downtown outlets were among the first to go. The suburban stores slowly died out during the late 1970s and 1980s, usually taken over by one or another of the various competing cafeteria chains that had come along in their wake.

While Britling was the most pervasive name in downtown eating, there were other grazing spots to tempt the taste buds. John's Restaurant opened in 1944 and, nearly seventy years later, was still flashing its theater-style marquee over Twenty-First Street. Of similar vintage was the La Paree on Fifth Avenue, in the heart of the hotel district, but it packed up its cuisine and quit at the end of 2003. A Shoney's Big Boy raised its fiberglass fat kid "with checkered overalls and Reagan hair," as one jokester put it, over the

Like some celebrities of the present day, a few downtown businesses were famous simply for being famous. Epp's Jewelers, on the corner of Second Avenue and Nineteenth Street across from Pizitz, was known for owner Taft Epstein's offbeat television antics, such as sponsoring the weekly wrestling matches and advertising with a toy monkey banging its cymbals.

entrance to the former Porter's clothing store at the corner of Third Avenue and Twentieth Street in 1967. Scores of smaller restaurants, such as the 1925 Pete's Hot Dogs on Second Avenue and other hot dog stands all over downtown, proved to be the relish on top of the rest.

For those who craved seafood at a reasonable price, there was Catfish King on Third Avenue, across the street from the Holiday Inn. It was the last manifestation of a local chain that had begun around 1959 with locations in Ensley and North Birmingham. By the late 1960s, the downtown location had joined the fun, along with an outlet in Woodlawn that operated out of a former funeral parlor—a most appetizing spot for wolfing down deep-fried southern cooking, right?

Catfish King was notable as much for its signage as for its food, subscribing firmly to the "every-surface-a-billboard" school of roadside architecture. The menu specials and their prices were splashed all over the building's exterior in loud yellow and red, and even louder was the neon sign depicting a leaping blue catfish with a glowing golden crown. The downtown Catfish King closed in the late 1970s, but a few of the other locations managed to swim along for a few more years. The Third Avenue building, stripped to its bare fish bones and rebuilt, eventually became the home of Jim Burke Nissan.

Chapter 5

BIRMINGHAM'S $1.5 MILLION CHRISTMAS GIFT

The young man craned his neck in the cold December air, trying to take in the sign flashing above him. He stepped back, watching as the seven letters "A-L-A-B-A-M-A" glowed in the night sky, the word they formed surrounded by a sea of other lights, all twinkling in a fiery circle.

"Alabama," the boy said under his breath, watching as the word came out in a vapor on the chilly air. "I've never seen anything like it."

Tommy Black, Birmingham News
October 11, 1980

The above scene, described so eloquently by *News* writer Black, was admittedly imaginary, but it could have happened. When Birmingham residents saw the opulence of the Alabama Theatre for the first time in the last week of 1927, all of a sudden, the other theaters that lined Second and Third Avenues were made to look like a nickel—or a nickelodeon, as the case may be.

The reason the Alabama outshone its brethren can be directly attributed to the status of its original owner, Paramount Studios. In those early days of the movies, studios were able to grow as powerful as they did because they not only produced the films, but they also owned the theaters where those pictures were shown. Paramount was no different, and by the 1920s, it had its own division known as Publix Theaters. The Paramount-Publix theaters were among the most elaborate movie palaces ever built during the latter half of the 1920s; the company's flagship was the gigantic Paramount Theater in New York City, opened in 1926.

The general public was first made aware of Paramount-Publix's plans for Birmingham during the summer of 1926. In response to an inquiry made by the *Birmingham News*, Harold Franklin, vice-president of Publix in New York, issued the following official statement:

> *Our company is erecting a theater and building at Third Avenue and Eighteenth Street which, when completed, will represent an investment of approximately $1,000,000. The theater is being designed by Graven & Magyer of Chicago, and will seat 3,000 persons. It will be unique in the fact that it will have a mezzanine floor containing exclusive loge seats. Outside of the theater entrance, the frontal of the Third Avenue and Eighteenth Street sides will contain shop fronts. The theater will have a front lobby three stories in height and luxurious public rooms. The theater will be equipped so that it can accommodate any type of attraction.*

As with any large undertaking, there were obstacles to be overcome. Paramount-Publix originally wanted its new movie palace to occupy the entire space between the Loveman, Joseph & Loeb department store building and Eighteenth Street, but the occupants of the building on the corner had a long-term lease and were not willing to surrender it unless they were paid a large bonus. For this reason, the Alabama was built in the shape of an L, with the entrance on Third Avenue and patrons then having to make a sharp right turn into the main auditorium, which backed up into Eighteenth Street. (Many decades later, the Alabama would have the last laugh on its obstinate corner occupants, as we shall see.)

Another change from the original plans had to do with the height of the structure. Paramount-Publix intended for the Alabama Theatre building to be seven stories tall, with neighbor Loveman's sharing space on the upper floors. This proved to be unworkable, and a good thing, too, since within a few years the Loveman building would burn to the ground, and it would have spelled disaster for the Alabama if the two had been joined at the shoulder.

Work on the building began in March 1927, and it progressed steadily. By September 28, the newspaper was announcing that the Alabama would be ready to open by December 15. They didn't quite make that date but came close. The estimated cost had ballooned from the original million to $1.25 million, and the newspaper further reported:

> *The feature Paramount picture will be accompanied by a special presentation similar to those of Flo Ziegfield, Frank Cambria, and others.*

The incredible Alabama Theatre opened the day after Christmas in 1927. When this photo was taken the following year, the feature attraction was *Wings*, noted as the first movie to win an Academy Award as Best Picture.

> *Artists booked for the Publix theaters' circuit will appear here, among them Paul Whiteman and other notables.*

Buried down in the description of all the theater's amenities, including a pianist on the mezzanine who would play requests from the customers, was a reference that today seems pitifully small considering the role it was to play in securing the building's future: "The organ will be one of the finest in the South and a famous organist will be here to demonstrate it on opening week. It was built according to the specifications of Jesse Crawford, organist known to all purchasers of phonograph records."

At last, the big day came. In fact, two big days came. Sunday, December 25, 1927, was Christmas Day, and the following afternoon, the Alabama Theatre had its formal grand opening. The timing of these two events was a boon for the newspaper writers, who trumpeted the event as "Birmingham Gets $1,500,000 Christmas Gift in Alabama Theatre." (Apparently the cost had made another jump.) A style of newspaper writing seldom seen anymore is demonstrated in the opening paragraphs by *Birmingham News* writer Dolly Dalrymple, who positively gushed:

> *When "Miss Birmingham" awoke this Christmas morn in the year of 1927, and gazed into her silk stocking hung gracefully by the municipal fireside, her eyes opened wide in amazement, her heart expanded largely, and her joy knew no bounds for, ensconced in that delectable hiding place was a gift which few cities can boast of and of which this city is eminently proud.*
>
> *Namely—a magnificent $1,500,000 theater, the gift of that splendid organization known as the Publix Theaters Corporation, which, realizing Birmingham's colorful past, her magnificent present and her roseate future ever progressing, ever growing, has put "the big pot in the little one" and spread itself all over the face of the earth in giving to the Magic City the newest, the most modern, the most artistic and the most comfortable theater that money and talent can devise.*

While Ms. Dalrymple takes an aspirin and rests on the couch to recover from her initial euphoria, let's throw open the doors of the Alabama and see what all the breathlessness was about. Without a doubt, it was unlike anything Birminghamians had ever seen. Making an entrance into the lobby, they were first confronted by the two-story Hall of Mirrors (instead of three stories as originally planned). Moving into the main lobby, visitors were surrounded by antique furniture and art objects purchased by Paramount from a castle in Spain and subsequently divided between Publix theaters in Los Angeles, New York and their new southern buddy, Birmingham. To reach the mezzanine or balcony required a strenuous climb up some imposing staircases, but those with lazier constitutions could enter the main auditorium on the ground floor, passing through wrought-iron gates constructed entirely from repetitions of the letter *A* (for Alabama, of course) in a variety of configurations.

That main auditorium was enough to make even the most jaded Birmingham moviegoer gasp. Five stories tall at its highest point, the theater had seating for 2,500 patrons, and the last row of the top balcony was 180 feet from the movie screen. The stage was equipped with an orchestra pit, and another pit that contained (when not in use) the Mighty Wurlitzer pipe organ. Modern-day movie buffs may have a tendency to forget that, for all its splendor, the Alabama Theatre was built to show silent movies. It was traditional in those days for the theater orchestra to provide the accompaniment for movies during nighttime performances, while for matinees the organ alone had to take the place of the higher-priced orchestra. At first glance, it appeared that there were box seats available near the stage on either side of the proscenium arch, but these were nothing but cleverly designed disguises for the chambers that held the massive ranks of pipes that gave the Wurlitzer the "mighty" part of its name.

Outside the auditorium, customers would find a multitude of other comforts that would far exceed anything they might have at home. There were men's and women's lounges, each of which was decorated in a scheme to make it different from the others: the ladies' lounge on the balcony resembled a Chinese tea room, while the one on the main floor went after a Spanish feel. The men's lounges were decorated as a circa 1488 Tudor manor (balcony) and an old English hunting lodge (ground floor). The theater was air conditioned, but not in the form as we know the term today. The 1927 definition of air-conditioning involved an elaborate system of circulating the stale air from the auditorium into a series of ducts that opened to the outside, while fresh air was pumped in from the ceiling. When cool air was needed during the summer months, the circulating air was blown over ice manufactured by a huge apparatus in the basement.

From the time of its opening, the Alabama became the premier theater of Birmingham, as it was intended to be. It is said that Paramount Pictures chief Adolph Zukor himself gave the edifice its nickname when he visited in person. "The Alabama Theatre is the Showplace of the South," he is reported to have commented, and that slogan stuck with the building forever after.

In 1931, Stanleigh Malotte arrived at the Alabama to begin serving as organist, a position he would hold until the late 1950s. Unfortunately, of that more than twenty-five-year career, only one recording of Malotte's organ technique is known to have survived. During the 1940s, Malotte divided his time between the theater and radio station WAPI, and a short Malotte

Stan Malotte arrived as the Alabama Theatre's organist in the early 1930s and remained for the better part of the next twenty years. Malotte's flamboyant style made him a natural showman and a highly anticipated part of any Alabama program.

radio program that happened to be preserved on a transcription disc is the only evidence of his voice and playing style. In this 1944 recording, he demonstrates some of the comedy and humorous musical sound effects for which he was famous and ends with a brief rendition of his theme song, "Stars Fell on Alabama," an oblique reference to his theater work. In later years, Malotte described his formula for entertaining audiences: "I play loud, I move around a lot, I use a lot of bells, and end with a patriotic song. You just can't go wrong doing that."

Around the time Malotte arrived at the Alabama, the playhouse became the weekly Saturday meeting spot for local boys and girls who were members of the Mickey Mouse Club. This was a promotion dreamed up by that impossible dreamer Walt Disney and instituted in movie theaters across the nation. From Orlando to Anaheim, kids gathered at their local showplaces to watch Disney cartoons (naturally), play games and see amateur talent shows, all the while squeaking the club slogan:

> *Handy! Dandy! Sweet as candy!*
> *Happy kids are we!*
> *Eenie! Ickie! Minnie! Mickey!*
> *M-O-U-S-E!*

Things were no different in Birmingham, although the Alabama did claim at one time the distinction of having the largest Mickey Mouse Club in the world, numbering some ten thousand junior Mickeys. The ringleader of the rat pack during the 1930s was the theater's assistant manager, George Neleans, who was known to the kids as "Grandpa Mickey Mouse." The *Birmingham News* reported on how "Grandpa" managed to keep any sort of discipline among the two thousand–plus youngsters who crowded into the theater every Saturday:

> *Occasionally some older members begin booing and hissing a performance. Grandpa Mickey Mouse halts all proceedings. "Now fellows," he says, "there are some people in here who don't like what we are doing. I want everybody here who disapproves of what these people are doing to hold up his hand." Every hand goes up, and you can bet that all disturbances are over for the day.*

For a while, the weekly shenanigans were broadcast over WBRC radio. Local stores, such as Pizitz, Sears and Loveman's, provided prizes to be given away, for which they received the thanks of being known as "Big Brother Mickey Mice." In March 1934, however, the weekly Mickey Mouse Club meeting was interrupted by a gift from Loveman's that the department store would have preferred not to give. During the afternoon performance, a fire quickly engulfed the entire 1899 building. Parents who had left their children

It is often forgotten that through much of its history, the Alabama Theatre had two identical versions of its huge vertical sign, one over the marquee and the other on the Eighteenth Street side of the building. The second sign later ended up stored in the basement, but it eventually disappeared into an uncertain fate.

in the care of Mickey and his cartoon and human friends were understandably hysterical, but fortunately a thirty-six-inch firewall separated the department store's annex building from the Alabama, so while Loveman's burned to the ground, the theater remained intact with only a bit of smoke damage. When the new Loveman's building was constructed on the spot where the old one had stood, a passageway was made from the top floor of the Alabama into the employees' lounge of the annex, and the two establishments would share their joys and sorrows forever after.

(While on the subject of Mickey, it might be worth noting here that Stan Malotte's brother Albert was a well-known composer, having crafted the most popular musical setting for "The Lord's Prayer." During the 1930s, Albert also created musical scores for a number of Walt Disney cartoons; thus, there were no doubt occasions during the Mickey Mouse Club meetings when Stan was performing live while his own brother's music was heard on the screen.)

Behind the scenes, events were taking place in the movie world that would affect the Alabama's future. The first came when the federal government decreed that the longstanding tradition of movie studios owning their own theaters, thereby controlling which pictures could be shown in them, constituted a monopoly. Paramount-Publix was forced to surrender the Alabama to Wilby-Kincey, an Atlanta-based company that operated theaters across the South. Later, Wilby-Kincey would sell the Alabama (and its nearby neighbor, the Ritz) to the ABC television network, an ironic twist if there ever was one.

Despite revolving ownerships, the Alabama Theatre remained virtually unchanged from its opening right up to the early 1960s. The most significant alteration made during that long span of time was the installation of a modernized air-conditioning system in 1952. The exterior of the theater was noticeably changed in May 1960, when manager Cecil McGlohon oversaw the erection of a new marquee that completely replaced the original 1927 masterpiece. Whereas the "old" marquee contained hundreds of screw-in light bulbs and featured the "ALABAMA" logo prominently (at one time, it also had a panel boasting "A PUBLIX THEATER"), the new marquee was lighted from within by neon tubing, with horizontal bands of "chasing" bulbs above and below.

During the same period, the Alabama served as the annual home for the Miss Alabama beauty pageant, all the while keeping up its program of movies and live stage shows. It also continued its tradition as a Saturday meeting place for kids, even though Walt Disney had long since pulled the Mickey Mouse Club out of the theater realm and turned it into a television program. The new sponsor of the weekly assembly was Guaranty Savings and Loan, which used the Alabama as home base for its promotion designed to get kids started banking with Guaranty at an early age, the "Flying G Savers Club." Now television was the main form of advertising, and the Flying G Savers Club was pushed heavily by such Birmingham kids' TV personalities as Cousin Cliff Holman, Benny Carle and Bozo the Clown. Regularly scheduled "show parties" were held at the Alabama, for which the only required admission price was that the children had to have a savings account with Guaranty. The local businesses such as Newberry's, Vaughan-Weil and Morrison's Cafeteria held up their end of the deal by continuing to provide prizes.

By 1972, trouble was just beginning to show its ugly face around the Alabama. In a valiant effort to keep the old-fashioned theater from looking too outdated, a total facelift was completed in February of that year. New red carpet, drapes and curtains (including a new stage curtain) were installed, and the main floor of the auditorium was fitted with new, roomier seats and wider aisles. This reduced the seating capacity of the main floor from

The management of the Alabama Theatre has said for years that "the show begins in the lobby." Sometimes that was taken literally, such as when WSGN's Tommy Charles broadcast his radio show in his pajamas, probably to promote Doris Day's movie *Pillow Talk* (1959).

1,200 to 923. The balcony retained its original 1927 carpet and, in fact, was frequently closed to the public when the demand for the extra seating was not so great. The last big event to take place during the Alabama's first life was the 1973 Birmingham premiere of *The Godfather*. After all that hoopla, things began a rapid downward spiral.

By 1978, current ABC Theaters manager Cecil Brown was squashing persistent rumors that the Alabama was in serious trouble. The downtown institution was subsisting on programs for school children and ladies' shopping matinees, while its nighttime business dropped off as the neighborhood around the theater slowly decayed. In fact, by that time, the Alabama was the only operating downtown theater that had not been reduced to showing greasy exploitation features. (As we shall see a few pages from now, the Ritz was closed, the Lyric was being used as the "Foxy Adult Cinema" and the Empire and Melba were wallowing in sleaze of the not-quite-X-rated variety.) The *Birmingham News* could see that the vultures were beginning to circle over the Alabama's marquee; in a sinister tone, the newspaper leered: "For some, the queen may look more attractive dead than alive. The building sits on very valuable land. And the materials used in construction—such as the gold leaf—could bring a small fortune on the market."

Such thoughts were enough to send a shiver down the Alabama's huge vertical sign. To ward off possible future trouble, during 1978, the theater was placed on the National Register of Historic Places. However, as the *News* morbidly reminded everyone, "That won't guarantee its existence, but it will require that some consideration be given to any such drastic action as tearing the building down."

Things didn't get any better. Later that year, ABC Theaters sold its giant-sized millstone to the Plitt Theater chain, which decided to spend the autumn of 1980 showing classic movies at the Alabama instead of trying to attract current hits. The rest of Third Avenue continued its steady decline, and the April 1980 closing of Loveman's made the Alabama seem like the old kid on the block. During this bleak period in the theater's history, the Mighty Wurlitzer was practically ignored by the public, but not by members of the Alabama Chapter of the American Theater Organ Society (ATOS), who worked tirelessly to be sure the magnificent instrument was kept in some sort of working order. What was going to become of the physical structure that housed the organ was not their primary concern—at least not at that particular time.

Once the series of classic films had ended, it appeared that so had the story of the Alabama Theatre. In the spring of 1981, the "Showplace of the South" was locked, the only human beings allowed inside being the ATOS members, who continued to try to keep the Wurlitzer from crumbling into ruin. Things looked a bit more hopeful in 1982, when developers Nelson

Head of Birmingham and Pedro Costa of Uruguay bought the Alabama, along with several other downtown buildings, as part of a giant-scale effort to revitalize the former theater and retail district. Costa and Head never got around to doing anything with the Alabama, but their ownership of it almost spelled its doom.

During the Costa-Head days, the ATOS Alabama Chapter would occasionally lease the theater for organ recitals and other such activities. Leading the charge in the drive to keep the theater afloat was Cecil Whitmire, who had arrived in Birmingham after a long run as organist at the Tennessee Theatre in Knoxville and who had become the Alabama's organist in 1977 for lack of anyone else who wanted the position. From May to October 1986, the group embarked on its most ambitious fundraising campaign yet: as the previous owners had done, a series of classic movies was shown at the Alabama. This was enough of a success that fifteen more cinema classics were scheduled for October 1986 through April 1987.

Changing times weren't finished with the Alabama yet, though. The winter/spring film series was a decided disaster attendance-wise, with some of the films attracting fewer than seventy people per showing. Whitmire and his hardy crew of volunteers knew that rough times were ahead: "We can't sell nostalgia forever," he reasoned. "We have to generate a new audience for the theater." Making matters worse was the fact that the Costa-Head partnership—the Alabama's legal owner—had filed for bankruptcy in June 1986. This meant that to keep the theater open at all, ATOS had to foot the ten-thousand-dollar-per-month bill of maintaining the building.

Desperate times call for desperate measures, and in March 1987, ATOS announced that it intended to buy the Alabama from the failed Costa-Head partnership for $1 million. This began a complicated series of maneuvers that ended up with ATOS making a $100,000 down payment on the building. Realizing that unless they were able to gain complete control of the theater its future would be in doubt, Whitmire used the news media to take his group's case to the public.

There had long been a sore spot in Birmingham over the 1969 demolition of the magnificent railroad terminal on Fifth Avenue, and ATOS used that infamous event as a reference point. Whitmire took that scar in historical preservation, ripped off the scab and made it into a festering boil, emphasizing that the same thing would happen to the Alabama Theatre if the necessary funds were not raised. His tactics pushed all the right buttons for the public, and ATOS collected more than the amount needed for the down payment. By allowing Costa and Head to retain parts of the building as office space, the total cost was reduced from $1 million to $777,000.

By 1990, ATOS had been replaced as the Alabama's operator by Birmingham Landmarks, Inc., a new nonprofit organization Whitmire began in order to more accurately reflect what was being done. Fundraising was progressing steadily, although Whitmire was relieved that he no longer had to whip Birmingham's nostalgic consciousness into such a frenzy. ("In fundraising, you can only cry wolf one or two times," he said, "and when you do, the wolf had better be there.")

The mortgage on the building hung over Birmingham Landmarks's head like the ornate domed ceiling in the Alabama's auditorium, but donations and pledges were coming in on a regular basis. Even Stan Malotte, who had passed away in 1972 after having spent most of his post-Alabama years at the Fox Theatre in Atlanta, was able to help his alma mater. Theater organist and historian John W. Langdon of Kentucky had somehow come into possession of the 1944 recording of Malotte's radio broadcast, and he in turn donated it to an Alabama-based radio organization, the National Lum and Abner Society. This group made the Malotte performance available to the Alabama Theatre, which sold cassette tapes of the broadcast for $25 each as part of its fundraiser. One of these tapes found its way to Malotte's son, Stan Jr. He traveled from his home in California to Birmingham to make a rare appearance at the unveiling of a star in his father's honor on the sidewalk in front of the theater.

It was in 1992 that the Alabama finally managed to buy the building on the corner of Third Avenue and Eighteenth Street that had been the holdout when the property was originally purchased in 1926, by then known as the Goldstein Furs building. At the same time, the Alabama began taking more steps to become a true performing arts center rather than simply a museum of the past. A bar was installed on the mezzanine level, to be used during suitable events. By now, the classic films that had brought attention back to the theater were relegated to summer showings, as that was traditionally the slowest time of year for live stage shows.

Under the direction of Whitmire and Birmingham Landmarks, the Alabama underwent a complete renovation, and there never seemed to be an end to the plans for the future. By the time Cecil Whitmire died on August 22, 2010, the theater and Birmingham Landmarks were on firm financial grounds and operated by a staff that would have been unthinkable during that bleak period when just unlocking the doors depended totally on volunteer efforts. Out of all the retail establishments and theaters that operated in downtown Birmingham over the years, the Alabama Theatre may be the only one that has managed to survive in anything resembling its original form and function. If a single business had to do it, the Alabama would probably be the best choice for the job.

Chapter 6

VAUDEVILLE DIES ON STAGE

Now, of course, the Alabama was not the last theater to be built in Birmingham, and it was not the first by a long shot. At one point, the Birmingham Historical Society came up with a count of seventy-three theaters that had operated in downtown Birmingham over the years, but of that number, only about a dozen made any sort of lasting impression in the public's memory. Most of the ones opened prior to the mid-1920s were not even built with movies as their first choice for entertainment, although many of them ended up with films on the bill.

One that never did was the Jefferson Theatre, which opened on Second Avenue in March 1900. The new playhouse, contrary to what one might presume, was not named after either Thomas Jefferson or Jefferson Davis. Instead, the Jefferson Theatre received its name from a famed stage actor of the day, Joseph Jefferson, whose most renowned performance was as the title character in *Rip Van Winkle*. It is assumed that his act did not put the audience to sleep, as he returned to Birmingham several times and even had his portrait hanging over the proscenium of the theater bearing his name.

Over the years, several people who actually witnessed performances at the Jefferson recorded their memories for posterity. In 1960, stage hand Henry Holtam told the *Birmingham News* about one of his most vivid recollections: "*Ben-Hur* was the most spectacular show that ever played [at] the Jefferson…They used two treadmills in the chariot race and they had four horses abreast and revolving scenery in the background…It took more scenery than any other show that ever came to Birmingham until *My Fair Lady*."

Birmingham's most celebrated live-performance theater of the early years of the twentieth century was the Jefferson. By the time of this view of Second Avenue, it had become known as the Erlanger (far left) and no longer seemed to stand out among its neighbors, Pizitz and the Ritz Theater.

Another well-known traveling stage show that played at the Jefferson was *Peter Pan*, starring Maude Adams. This play made its biggest impact on show business history far north of Birmingham, though, as Ms. Adams and her troupe passed through Missouri around the same time and made a huge impression on an imaginative local youngster named Walt Disney. He would later produce a movie or two that would supply product for the downtown Birmingham theaters, but that's another story.

The days of high society going out to a traveling stage show were eventually eclipsed by the rise of first vaudeville and then motion pictures. At some point, the Jefferson became the local outlet for the Klaw-Erlanger vaudeville circuit, and the name was changed to the Erlanger Theatre for a while. That era came to a close as well, and the rotting old Jefferson building was razed in the summer of 1946 to make way for a parking lot, which in turn made way for an addition to the Phoenix Building.

One of the Jefferson's contemporaries was originally built in 1890 as a civic auditorium (long before the Boutwell Auditorium, long before

Mayor Boutwell was even born, in fact!). Located on the northwest corner of Third Avenue and Seventeenth Street, the auditorium was converted into the Bijou Theatre in 1898, and within a few years, it was one of the premier Birmingham outlets for touring vaudeville companies. The aforementioned Henry Holtam recalled that the Bijou was so popular that it held performances six nights a week and three matinees, all accompanied by an eight-piece orchestra. As with the Jefferson, many performers appeared at the Bijou during either the height of their popularity or on their way to greater fame. Among those in the latter category was legendary song-and-dance man George M. Cohan, who performed at the Bijou in 1903.

According to newspaper reports, in 1915, the Bijou closed and two years later reopened as part of the Loew's vaudeville circuit. *Birmingham News* columnist Lane Carter wrote, "Old-timers may remember when Marcus Loew brought a circus to the Bijou every year. There were real wild animal acts, and the lobby was all dressed up like a real circus. Candy and popcorn were sold. A midget show was also booked into the Bijou once a year, and every kid in town filled the house." As we shall see later in this chapter, the Bijou was eventually purchased by another vaudeville circuit and became known as the Pantages, but let's not count our theater tickets before they're sold.

Meanwhile, on the opposite corner from the Bijou stood the Orpheum Theatre. It had originally been built as a skating rink but became a vaudeville house in 1908. It remained in this form for only four years, after which it was converted into a garage and was later demolished. Of all the early theaters, the Orpheum seems to be the only one for which no photographic record was ever made. Ironically, though, more of it survives today than many of its better-documented relatives. The site of the Orpheum is a parking lot, and the retaining bricks around the side and back of the lot are actually the lower portions of the Orpheum's former walls. The Bijou and the Jefferson have left no such monuments to their existences.

The Majestic was another theater that started out with stage performances and ended up as a vaudeville venue. Located on Third Avenue across from the spot where the Alabama Theatre would be built many years later, the Majestic opened in 1905 and converted to vaudeville in 1913. Among the acts appearing there was a bug-eyed teenager named Eddie Cantor, who would go on to bigger and better things. Amazingly, the building that housed the Majestic still stands. For most of the years since the 1920s, it served as a furniture store of one brand or another, with seemingly no remnant of its days as a vaudeville theater.

THE JEFFERSON

Tuesday, Matinee and Night, Oct. 2

MURRAY AND MACK

In Their Successful Musical Farce

AROUND THE TOWN

40——PEOPLE——40

NEW SONGS, NEW DANCES AND PRETTY GIRLS

Thursday, Matinee and Night, Oct. 4

FLORENCE DAVIS

A Company of Well-known New York Players, in the Exquisite Romantic Comedy

THE PLAYER MAID

Friday, October 5

WRESTLING MATCH

BURNS vs. GIANT DANE

Seats at Box Office 3 days ahead

Saturday, Matinee and Night, Oct. 6

45 MINUTES FROM BROADWAY

A musical play in three acts by GEO. M. COHAN
Under the business direction of Cohan & Harris

THE BIJOU

THORNS AND ORANGE BLOSSOMS

Matinees Tuesday, Thursday and Saturday

MAJESTIC THEATRE

"Pals"

The $5,000.00 production that has proven a sensation in vaudeville. A car load of special scenery and the Original New York Cast.

Jeanette Laurelle

The Parisian Marvel in the beautiful "Le Ciel."

Lew Wells

The King of Monologue and Saxaphone Eccentricities.

Veolette and Old

Telepathy Mind Reading.

Belle Gordon

The Champion Girl Bag Puncher.

De-Coe

The "Ten-Story" Man.

MATINEE EVERY DAY

THE NEW GAYETY

ALL WEEK—LADIES' MATINEE DAILY

Bachelors' Club Burlesquers

Catchy Music——New Songs
Pretty Girls

SKATING RINK

On Avenue F and 24th Street

Opens and offers to the devotees of this sport the finest skating surface and best skates in the South

The status of Birmingham's theater scene in October 1906 can be quickly digested by studying this handbill promoting the acts that were treading the boards that week.

Even more so than the early movie theaters, the vaudeville theaters that did not survive to host that new medium are mostly forgotten today. Among others on Third Avenue were the Alamo and the Victoria, with the Amuse-U and the Vaudette holding down the fort on Second Avenue. For those with slightly less refined tastes, the Gayety Theatre at the corner of First Avenue and Nineteenth Street was a burlesque house with a rich history. The building had been constructed in 1882 as O'Brien's Opera House but lost its prestige when the traveling shows moved to the Jefferson in 1900.

Under its assumed name as the Gayety, the faded beauty managed to hold on until 1910, and it was razed five years later. Bricks from the demolished theater were used to build a retail block on that site, with a historical marker explaining its significance. At some point in the 1980s, even that structure was demolished, and now no one seems to know the fate of O'Brien's bricks or even the sign that told their story. As the old saying goes, that's show biz.

All the preceding bright lights of the Birmingham theater community were forced to bow their heads when the grandest vaudeville house of them all, the Lyric Theatre, came to town. For some reason, an opening date of 1912 became attached to the Lyric in its later years, and it was only through the diligent research of Cecil Whitmire that the true opening of January 11, 1914, was established. That two-year discrepancy did not matter much in the long run, as the Lyric would have shamed the earlier theaters no matter when it opened. Built for the prestigious Keith vaudeville circuit, the Lyric sported ornate balconies and wall ornamentation and, from its opening day, featured some of the biggest acts on the road. On opening night, the headliner was cartoonist Rube Goldberg, and he was soon followed by another famous gagman, Bud Fisher of the *Mutt and Jeff* comic strip. Others who played at the Lyric during its first life were Will Rogers, Sophie Tucker, the Marx Brothers, Jack Benny and Fred Allen.

After the arrival of the Lyric, the older vaudeville theaters began closing up one by one. The repertory company from the Jefferson Theatre transferred its allegiance to the Lyric, where it became known as the Favorite Players. The Eighteenth Street side of the Lyric building bears a sign painted on the brick that advertises this troupe. For years, it was so faded as to be barely legible, but thanks to the efforts of Birmingham Landmarks, it has now been restored to something resembling its original appearance.

However, the combination of the dual arrival of the Great Depression and the double sock of radio and the movies rang a sour note for the Lyric. In late 1930 or early 1931, it closed its doors as a vaudeville theater and reopened in April 1932 strictly as a movie house. (Just to indicate how show business was changing, the Keith vaudeville circuit had eventually merged with the Orpheum circuit to become known as Keith-Orpheum. This entity then hooked up with David Sarnoff, head of the NBC radio network, to form a new movie studio known as Radio-Keith-Orpheum, or RKO Radio Pictures. The movies were winning; there was no doubt of that.)

The Lyric was Birmingham's most lavish vaudeville theater when it opened in 1914. The lobby was a work of art, but in later years, it was hidden behind sheetrock walls and acoustic tile drop ceilings. The insert shows how the original 1914 fixtures were uncovered in the 1980s once the first attempts at renovation began.

Those who have taken on the responsibility of preserving the Lyric and its history are fond of pointing out one of its unique characteristics. In the days of segregation, the Lyric had a separate "colored balcony" for nonwhite customers. This meant it was one of the few venues in Birmingham where African American theatergoers could watch a performance at the same time as white customers, restricted though they might have been. (Most theaters, including the Alabama, allowed no African American audiences at all, anytime or anywhere.) The Lyric survived on showing second-run features that had already played the other downtown theaters until it was closed again, this time in either 1958 or 1960, depending on what source one consults. In any case, it looked like the end had come.

Around 1964 there was some talk of renovating the Lyric, but nothing happened until 1973, when a couple of Jefferson State Junior College pals and old movie buffs, Dee Sloan and Robert Horton, got the bright idea to reopen the Lyric to show classic movies of bygone eras. Rather than keeping the Lyric name, which had no doubt become tarnished from its years as a second-rate showplace, Sloan and Horton redubbed it the Grand Bijou and set about to show such cinema milestones as *The Jazz Singer* and classics starring W.C. Fields and the Marx Brothers (who, after all, had actually appeared there in person decades ago). While preparing the old theater to come back to life, the new movie moguls discovered that underneath the main floor was an enormous tank that could have been used for staging such vaudeville spectaculars as Billy Rose's "Aquacade," although there was no evidence that water acts of that type had ever been presented there.

Unfortunately, the novelty of showing nothing but antique movies wore off after a year, and the Lyric shuddered in the face of its new identity: the Foxy Adult Cinema. This questionable personality persisted through the late 1970s and into the early 1980s before even pornography was not enough to lure people into the aging structure.

The Lyric got its brightest prospect for the future yet when the building was purchased by Birmingham Landmarks, the company that had so successfully restored the Alabama Theatre. Plans were formulated to do the same for the Lyric once the proper funding was secured. Those efforts have been ongoing ever since, but have picked up speed over the last couple of years. One thing that has been made perfectly clear is that the Lyric is not being restored as a movie theater. The Alabama still serves that need when necessary, and the goal is to use the Lyric for live stage shows, its original function.

The Lyric's lobby had been "hiding in plain sight," as the expression goes, because after the theater's circa 1960 closing, that space had been converted into a store. (During its porno house days, patrons had entered through the Eighteenth Street doors, and most people eventually forgot there had ever been a lobby.) Finally, as finances permitted, the acoustic tile ceiling and drywalls were removed to reveal the original 1914 lobby architecture in all its splendor and in remarkably good shape, considering how long it had been neglected.

The same could be said for the Lyric's auditorium, although it too was quite a decayed mess when Birmingham Landmarks first got ahold of it. None of the Lyric's original marquees had survived, but in the fall of 2013, a new marquee that recreated the look of the 1914 one was proudly installed above the lobby-in-progress, a much-welcomed indicator that progress was being made. Although as of this writing it is too early to speculate, there were hopes that the Lyric might be reopened during its centennial year.

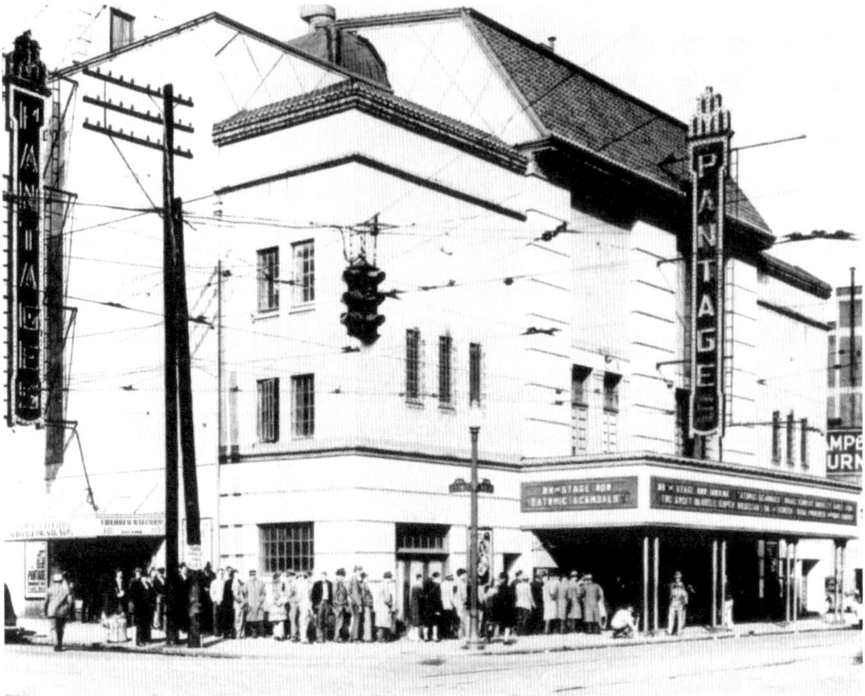

This theater was known as the Pantage in its advertisements, but the electric signs called it the Pantages. Either way, it survived into the late 1940s as Birmingham's last vaudeville house.

Even though vaudeville was a dying medium, around 1927 the Pantages circuit took over the former Bijou Theatre and completely remodeled it, leaving only the side and back walls and the stage as the originals. One aspect where someone forgot to do his job was in deciding what the name of the new theater was going to be. Newspaper articles and ads over the years consistently referred to it as the Pantage, whereas the electric signs in front read Pantages. Take your pick.

The Pantages continued presenting vaudeville shows and revues until 1946, when it was converted into an all-black theater, the Birmingham, which joined its nearby neighbors on Fourth Avenue, the Carver and the Famous, in catering to that often-neglected clientele. Even that did not last very long, and in the spring of 1950, the entire building was leveled for a parking lot.

It was Bob Hope (who undoubtedly appeared in at least one of the theaters we have mentioned at some point during his early career) who observed, "When vaudeville died, television was the box it was buried in." However,

Ads such as this one from 1943 demonstrate why "nice people" supposedly did not patronize the Pantages in its later years. (That probably did not stop a number of them from covertly attending these performances, though.)

the edifice that outlived all the others lasted well into the TV era before it too succumbed. When originally built, however, baggy-pants comics and torch singers were the last things intended for it.

In October 1921, President Warren G. Harding laid the cornerstone for what was to be the new Masonic temple at Fifth Avenue and Eighteenth Street. The auditorium was built in the style of an amphitheater and was used for Zamora Shrine ceremonies until 1925. That was the year the Loew's vaudeville circuit left what had once been the Bijou (and was on its way to becoming the Pantages), and the troupe moved into the Masonic hall, which was promptly, and appropriately, renamed the Temple Theatre.

More than any of the others, the Temple remained closest to its roots throughout its long history. Movies were shown there, but it remained first and foremost a performing arts facility, hosting big names such as Tallulah Bankhead, Maurice Evans, Helen Hayes, John Barrymore and many others. The stars might have been big, but one of the few sore points they found about the Temple was its relatively small stage. A *Birmingham News* magazine supplement reported: "The Temple stage has a depth of 22.6 feet. The ideal depth is 38 feet...When a big show like *South Pacific* came to the Temple, it wasn't possible to get all the scenery on the small stage, and some of the sets had to be parked in the alley until they were used."

Big sets and little stage notwithstanding, the Temple held on to its reputation right to the end. That came on March 31, 1970, when Metropolitan Opera star Jerome Hines became the final performer to appear at the Temple. There was enough advance publicity that everyone knew it was curtains for the venerable old theater, including Hines himself. "I'll be able to tell my manager in New York that we brought down the house," he wisecracked, although most of the audience probably failed to see any humor in the situation.

Chapter 7

THE MOVIES MOVE IN

The closing and subsequent demolition of the Temple Theatre occurred less than a year after a similar fate had befallen Birmingham's opulent railroad terminal station, so there was at least somewhat of a movement to preserve pieces of the old hall. The 2,400-pound chandelier that hung over the audience in the main auditorium was obtained by Samford University, and in 1976, it took up residence in the Wright Fine Arts Center on the university's campus. The Temple's red stage curtain and some of the seats were transplanted to the Fort Payne Opera House, so at least it survived in a piecemeal fashion long after the other theaters were gone with the wind.

Say, wasn't that the title of a famous movie? Why, sure it was, and not coincidentally, that weak transition lowers the lights for the next act in our downtown drama, the emergence of the motion picture houses.

Since for many years movies were considered the illegitimate offspring of the legitimate theater, their arrival in Birmingham went considerably more unnoticed than the goings-on behind the scenes at the more refined showplaces. However, through his own research of unknown sources, historian Malcolm C. MacMillan pinpointed in 1975 the first movie theater in Birmingham as the Theatorium, which he found opened on Twentieth Street on March 14, 1905. According to McMillan, "The film was projected against a barrel with a sheet for a screen, and often the only sound heard was kissing in the audience." (And people thought drive-in theaters had something new to offer in the post–World War II years!)

As this brief but evocative description would indicate, early movie theaters were opened with little attention paid to architecture or comfort. In most cases, they were simply converted retail space in which movies would be shown until the public grew tired of them. The Pastime Theatre, for example, occupied what had formerly been known as the Peerless Saloon, and the more upper-class Birminghamians probably felt there was little change in status when the building morphed from a saloon into a nickelodeon.

Of those first few years, the Birmingham Historical Society reported, "Eleven movie houses first appeared in city directories of 1908 with such names as Electric, Theatorium, Edisonia, Elite, Musetorium, Newsome, St. Nicholas, Alamo and Marvel, but only two survived the following years." The fact that these names are not the stuff of people's fond memories today indicates that their influence—indeed, their very existence—was somewhat short-lived.

For reasons now lost to time, the vast majority of the Birmingham movie theaters clustered along Second Avenue, primarily between Nineteenth and Twenty-First Streets, although there were exceptions. Among the "second wave" of more permanent silent theaters along this strip were the Galax, the Alcazar (later renamed the Capitol) and the Trianon.

As most film fans know, movies did not begin to talk until 1927, when Warner Bros. debuted its new "Vitaphone" system of synchronizing sound and picture with *The Jazz Singer*, starring Al Jolson. ("You ain't heard nothing yet" was not just his trademark line in the movie, but a good slogan for what was coming in the motion picture industry.) *The Jazz Singer* blew into Birmingham at the venerable Strand Theater, another member of the Second Avenue crowd but easily the most lavish of all the early silent-era theaters.

Just when the Strand opened is somewhat vague from the few historical references to it, but the theater was apparently built around 1914 on the spot formerly occupied by the Steele-Smith Dry Goods Company (and until 1890, the property had been the original Loveman, Joseph & Loeb store). From the beginning, it was obvious that the Strand was not going to be the same as the small storefront theaters that surrounded it. The Strand name was spelled out in mosaic tile above the marquee, and the façade of the building was suitably impressive in its ornamentation.

Whereas the biggest names in vaudeville were appearing on stage at the Lyric, the Bijou and their kin, it was at the Strand that the newly rising stars of motion pictures could usually be found when passing through Birmingham. Screen idol and future character actor Francis X. Bushman put in an appearance at the Strand and was almost mobbed by his fans. Clara

As movies supplanted vaudeville as the public's favorite entertainment, a string of motion picture theaters grew along both sides of Second Avenue. The site of the Strand and Capitol, along with many of their adjacent businesses, became a parking deck in the 1960s.

Kimball Young made a scene that wasn't in the script when she arrived and found the theater had no stage on which she could appear. The manager hastily fashioned a platform out of parallel boards covered with flowers, but it did little to mollify the actress's ruffled feathers.

As mentioned earlier, the biggest event in the Strand's history was when *The Jazz Singer* introduced the concept of talking pictures on its screen, running for an amazing thirteen weeks. It is said that people made the trip from as far away as Montevallo and Sylacauga just to see what a sound movie was.

By the 1940s, the Strand was still as opulent, but competition from the newer theaters had reduced it to showing second-run features and B-pictures. Its later history was intertwined with the theater next door, the Capitol (alias the Alcazar). In December 1948, the Capitol changed its name to the Newmar and also went into the business of showing features that had already appeared at the Alabama and Ritz theaters. This would have had little effect on the Strand, except that after a few years of this, the Newmar closed up and moved into the Strand building, taking the Newmar name with it. By that time, modernized marquees had all but hidden the original Strand mosaic logo, so most people probably did not think it strange to see two different names on a single building.

In September 1959 the Newmar name came down and the Strand marquee went up again, in time for the theater to reopen with Walt Disney's latest hit, *Darby O'Gill and the Little People*. The luck of the Irish would not remain with the Strand for long, though. On November 28, 1962, the Strand locked its doors after running the Vincent Price fright flick *Tower of London*, which some felt was an appropriate finish for the once glamorous edifice.

It stood abandoned until the following August, when the wrecking ball arrived to make room for a parking deck for the Birmingham Trust National Bank (BTNB). *Birmingham News* reporter Lane Carter had bittersweet memories of the Strand, reminiscing about how he attended a movie there on his very first day as a *News* employee. His closing remarks were eloquent:

> *As I walked by the old theater the other afternoon, and saw it coming to pieces, the name "Strand" breaking up like a beautiful dream fading as you wake, I got that hollow feeling that hits a man when he remembers his youth and the long ago; when the shadows across the silver screen were wonderful figures from a glamorous and remote world called Hollywood.*
>
> *I'll always remember the old Strand with that tug at my heartstrings. I don't care what they put in its place, a parking lot, or skyscraper, or even another theater. There'll always be a Strand Theatre standing there in my memory.*

The Trianon was one of the silent movie theaters that did not survive long after "talkies" came into being. This building still stands on Second Avenue, most recently (and unwittingly) carrying on a different form of its original function by selling movies on DVD.

Not all the theaters that survived from the silent era produced such an outpouring of nostalgia when they finally faded to black. Take the case of the Royal Theatre, for example. Small by anyone's standards, the Royal sat just a few doors west of the gigantic Comer building and, from its beginning to its end, specialized in one type of entertainment, and one type only: the hardy western.

Whether it was pioneer screen cowboys Tom Mix and Buck Jones or their latter-day descendants such as Gene Autry, Roy Rogers and Lash LaRue, they all found the Royal to be a royal hitching post. In the end, however, the Royal was not done in so much by its changing neighborhood and surroundings as by the one-eyed owl hoot that was invading everyone's living room, the TV set.

Television came to Birmingham in the summer of 1949 but, of course, had been gaining momentum in other parts of the country for several years. One of the effects this new medium had on the movie industry was a gradual reduction in the number of B-pictures (such as westerns) that were being churned out. For all practical purposes, there was very little difference between a B-Western and a television program, so they were among the first casualties in the movies-versus-TV war.

The Empire Theater on Third Avenue used this 1949 ad to show crowds standing in line, stretching westward past the Britling Cafeteria and around the corner of the Watts Building onto Twentieth Street.

With its only source of entertainment drying up like a water hole in Death Valley, the Royal hung up its ten-gallon hat and quit the trail in early 1951. This event did not make the newspapers, and many people were probably surprised to find the theater boarded up. After sitting unwanted and unwashed for a couple of years, the space formerly occupied by the Royal was leased as a Morrison's Cafeteria, and probably few people who ate there realized they were grazing where formerly the deer and the antelope had played. That was a discouraging word, to be sure.

While the smaller theaters such as the Royal were headin' 'em off at the pass on Second Avenue, up on Third Avenue, the Empire Theatre had opened in early 1927. The Empire represented a sort of hybrid of theater styles, being built for silent movies but also containing dressing rooms underneath the stage. Presumably it was hedging its bet on which entertainment medium would eventually prevail.

Although its longevity was notable, there seems to have been very little that was remarkable about the Empire's history. To read the newspaper articles about it, the Empire seems to have been in an almost constant state of reinventing itself. It managed to exist with its original decor and marquee for the first twenty-two years of its existence but underwent its first major remodeling program in the summer and fall of 1949. This had the effect of covering the front of the Empire's four-story building with "Permastone," a move that would not endear the structure to historical preservationists in the future. The new marquee was the type with interchangeable plastic letters, which also went a long way toward destroying any historic value the theater might have had.

Fifteen years later, in 1964, the Empire was remodeled again, enlarging practically every aspect of the structure. The screen inflated from twenty-four to thirty-five feet, while seats were ripped out and replaced with a larger "rocking chair" type, which took up more space and thus reduced the number of seats available on the main floor. When the Empire had its "open house" to unveil its new look in February 1965, the newspaper headlined the blurb, "Sign of downtown progress." It was not exactly so. Over the following ten years, both the neighborhood around the Empire and the quality of the movies shown there would go into a tailspin, as we will see a few pages from now. For the present, let it suffice to say that the Empire building was demolished in July 1984 with few tears shed by anyone; it and the site of the Britling Cafeteria that long stood next door are now a parking lot.

The mid- to late 1920s were the peak era of the "movie palace," those elaborate, richly appointed playhouses that made even the fanciest storefront theaters such as the Empire look plain. However, it is amazing to realize that in the time frame we have been discussing so far, Birmingham had not had anything that could truly be called a movie palace. A hint that things were about to change was dropped into newspaper readers' laps on September 27, 1925, when an article announced:

> *Birmingham's first motion picture palace will begin to be a reality about October 1, when construction will start on a million dollar theater at 1719–1723 Second Avenue North...Construction of the million dollar movie house marks another improvement in this section of Second Avenue. At Nineteenth Street, the second unit of the big Pizitz store is nearing completion. At Eighteenth Street, the new Herman Saks store is another addition. The final touches are being put on the five-story concrete building that will be the future home of Cain Brothers furniture, immediately adjoining the Jefferson Theatre. The erection of the Mudd-Colley house is held to mean a greater centralization of the theatrical center around Eighteenth Street and Second and Third Avenues. The Jefferson and Lyric are already open. The Mudd-Colley house will be ready in a few months and another big theater is planned for the same neighborhood.*

The Ritz Theater is prominent in this circa 1930 view of Second Avenue. The building with the tall, pointed tower is the old Birmingham post office, which was demolished in the early 1930s and later became the site of the Loveman's (now McWane Science Center) parking deck.

(In case your hindsight is a little nearsighted, the "other big theater" turned out to be the Alabama, but it would be a couple of years before it could steal the spotlight.)

Meanwhile, the new "million dollar" theater was given the name "Ritz" and an opening date of August 15, 1926. As was typical of the period, the silent movie that was the opening night feature (*More Pay, Less Work*, starring Mary Brian and Buddy Rogers) took second row to the acts presented on stage by the Keith-Orpheum vaudeville circuit. Star performers were New York musicians and comedians Herman and Sammy Timberg; Sammy would go on to make a bigger name for himself by writing the music for the Betty Boop and Popeye cartoons for the Max Fleischer animation studio during the 1930s.

Besides the New York performers, the Ritz also boasted Al Plante and his "Ritz Augmented Orchestra," and the twenty-five-thousand-dollar pipe organ that was a proud feature of any movie palace worth its gilt. According to the newspapers, tens of thousands of the local populace showed up at the Ritz on its Sunday afternoon open house, and of course, many of those returned to become regular customers over and over again in the future. If the articles used the phrase "million dollar theater" once, they used it a million times.

It is ironic that just as the Ritz was opening as the epitome of the theatergoing experience, the movie industry was experiencing the somewhat painful changeover from silent to sound pictures. When the Ritz eventually got a new manager in the personage of A.H. Talbot of Chicago, *Birmingham News* writer Dolly Dalrymple (whom we met in the Alabama Theatre discussion a couple of chapters ago) interviewed the new man with the company and filed these comments:

> *Especially during the last 10 years, when moving pictures have been raised to the dignity almost of legitimate performances, and practically all of the great actors of the legitimate stage have succumbed to the fascination of the "talkies," has this business or vocation taken on new life and new phases.*

Talbot then chimed in with his views on how this changing business of entertainment would continue to evolve:

> *Of course the talkies today are still in the infant stage and the end of them, well, no one can tell. One thing is certain and sure though, and that is they have come to stay. Television is the next link in the chain…I believe*

> *television will eventually be used exactly like the radio. People will sit in their own homes and hear and see the play without going to the theater for this purpose.*

If it sounds as though Talbot wasn't telling anyone anything they didn't already know, please take into consideration that his remarks were published in the paper on March 25, 1931. We're sure Talbot, with his keen foresight, must have made a bundle in the entertainment business, especially if he were smart enough to get out of theaters and into television.

For whatever reason, during the Ritz's long Birmingham stay, it became the theater of choice for testing out every new device or system the motion picture industry tried in order to get people away from that television menace manager Talbot had so eerily prophesied. Actually, even before that happened, the Ritz had undergone two major remodelings (1933 and 1940), but neither of them compared to the assault on the building's history that began in the late 1950s.

First there was Todd-AO. What's that, you ask? Todd-AO was the trade name of a new motion picture process that doubled the size of the image from 35mm to 70mm film and also involved the latest in high-fidelity sound. It was named in honor of producer Mike Todd, who introduced the "better than TV" format in his feature *Around the World in 80 Days*. Installation of the new, curved screen and the multitude of audio speakers required to produce the hi-fi sound decimated most of whatever was left of the Ritz's original structure and appearance. However, the theater spared no effort in proclaiming that it could now show such Todd-AO epics as *The Big Fisherman* and *Ben-Hur* (all of a sudden we're back where the Jefferson Theatre started).

Most amusing of all was the newspaper's remark that "Todd-AO has been described by reviewers as a 'practical version of Cinerama,' which, because of its tremendous installation and operational expense, has not been profitable for theater exhibitors except in the largest cities." With that established, wouldn't you know that the next major remodeling program at the Ritz was to turn it into the state's first Cinerama theater?

Yes, it's true. During the spring and early summer of 1962, the insides of the Ritz were ripped out and rebuilt again, this time to provide the multiple screens required by Cinerama, which had been trying to get people out of the TV-viewing habit and back into the theaters for almost ten years by that time. The novelty might have worn off in the rest of the movie industry, but Birmingham (and the Ritz) treated it as though it were the greatest

SKATELAND
ROLLER RINK

EXCITEMENT!
Luise RAINER
DeCORDOVA
Wm. BENDIX
Paul LUKAS
"HOSTAGES"
Strand

WHEN DEATH STRIKES
THE ZOMBIES WALK!
JOHN CARRADINE
"REVENGE OF THE ZOMBIES"
GALE STORM
ROBERT LOWERY
MANTAN MORELAND
BOB STEELE
STARTS TOMORROW!
GALAX

CAPITOL NOW!
"THE FEMININE TOUCH"
DON AMECHE
KAY FRANCIS
ROSALIND RUSSELL
AUTO MOVIES NO. 1
"HITLER'S CHILDREN"
On Bessemer Super Highway

ENSLEY
"BACKGROUND TO DANGER"
SEASON'S FIRST BROADWAY STAGE HIT!
"The DOUGHGIRLS"
TODAY
TEMPLE THEATER

AVON
NIGHT PLANE FROM CHUNGKING

4 Shows Daily
ON OUR STAGE
In Person
NAUGHTY BUT NICE
STARTS TOMORROW
PANTAGE

"MR. BIG'S" BACK...SO COME ON DOWN AND HOWL!
DONALD O'CONNOR
SUSANNA FOSTER
PEGGY RYAN
TOP MAN
RICHARD DIX • ANNE GWYNNE
COUNT BASIE
And His Orchestra
Musical and Latest War News
Starts TODAY!
the RITZ

The Peak of THRILLS
PACKED ADVENTURE!
WILD BILL ELLIOTT
WAGON TRACKS WEST
George "Gabby" HAYES
Tom TYLER
Anne JEFFREYS
Starts TOMORROW
ROYAL
"ARIZONA BOUND"

ALWAYS A Pleasure
COOK'S Imperial
America's Finest CHAMPAGNE

"BUTCH MINDS THE BABY"
"YOUNG AND WILLING"
"MARGIN FOR ERROR"
"Background to Danger"
"RHYTHM of the ISLANDS"
"FOLLOW THE BAND"
"BUTCH MINDS THE BABY"
"JOHNNY DOUGHBOY"
"JOHNNY DOUGHBOY"
"Quiet, Please—Murder"
"RHYTHM of the ISLANDS"

HELD OVER
2nd WEEK
SALUTE TO THE MARINES
WALLACE BEERY
FAY BAINTER • REGINALD OWEN
NOW
LYRIC

THREE GIRLS on His MIND!
One In His Heart ...
One In His Eye ...
One In His Hair ...
And All Three Know He's THE RIGHT MAN!
He'll Hit Any Man Who Needs It ...
He's A Hit To Three Women Who Need Him!
Alan LADD
Julie BISHOP
"The RIGHT MAN"
Edith FELLOWS • Wilbur EVANS
Roger DANIEL • Judith LINDEN
Marion KERBY • Marlo DWYER
EMPIRE
"Where the Crowds Go"
More Entertainment
"AIR CREW"
Latest Pathe News
Victory Short
FOOD and MAGIC
Starts TODAY

IT'S FROZEN FUN FOR THE DURATION!
SONJA SKATES...AS WOODY SERENADES!
It's hotter than a snowball in Hades...with romance, rhythm and revelry. It all happens on ice ...and it's happiness all the way!
SONJA HENIE
Wintertime
JACK OAKIE
CESAR ROMERO
CAROLE LANDIS
S. Z. Sakall · Cornel Wilde
WOODY HERMAN
and his Orchestra
One Week of Music and Fun, Beginning
TODAY
ALABAMA
"Show Place of the South"
More!
STANLEIGH MALOTTE
20th CENTURY-FOX PICTURE

The movies perhaps had their greatest popularity during World War II, when the nation needed entertainment and television was still confined to experimental laboratories. This page from a November 1943 newspaper shows that the downtown movie houses were all doing their bit to keep up the morale.

advancement in movies since Al Jolson. Buried down in all the publicity was the offhanded remark that up to that point, the only movies produced in the Cinerama format were travelogues. Thrilling as it might have been to take a simulated roller coaster ride or view the beauty of Florida's venerable Cypress Gardens in lifelike realism, moviegoers wanted stories, and the Ritz had to wait almost six months before the first (and some of the few) Cinerama movies with a plot were released.

The conversion to Cinerama really destroyed the Ritz's small remaining amount of historical value. The three screens took up the entire width of the front of the theater, requiring that the chambers that once housed the pipes of the twenty-five-thousand-dollar organ be unceremoniously closed off with cement blocks. The number of seats dropped dramatically, from 1,700 to 500. Even the Ritz's marquee received a Cinerama logo overlay, hiding the red-and-green neon tubes that truly looked as if they belonged to another era.

Ironically, within a couple of years, Cinerama also belonged to another era. By 1964, the Ritz was being remodeled yet again, this time to rid itself of Cinerama and get back to a more normal appearance. From that point onward, the Ritz seems to have given up "putting on the Ritz." After years of steadily declining attendance and interest, the old dinosaur coughed its last in 1977.

In 1982, the *Post-Herald* newspaper sent reporter Terry Horne down to Second Avenue to see if anything was left of the Ritz's faded glory. "The

In 1982, the Ritz Theater and most of the block in which it stood was demolished for a parking lot. This newspaper photo was taken just before the wrecking ball began to swing and also gives us a glimpse of Pasquale's Pizza on the corner.

green and red neon tubes are now caked with dust, the white tiled front chipped and cracked," Horne wrote. "Still tacked to the glass-covered boards are the coming attractions posters: a 1977 Richard Pryor movie, a 1975 Clint Eastwood movie, and a personal appearance by 'Wildman Steve,' a black X-rated comedian." (Somehow, it was good to know that even in this perverse way, the Ritz was still tentatively holding on to its origin as a vaudeville performance theater.)

There was no movement to rescue the Ritz from the wrecking ball, as had been done for the Alabama Theatre, because unlike the Alabama, there was not enough left of the Ritz's original structure to classify it as a historic building. Irony of ironies, all the remodeling it had seen to keep it up to date over the years had destroyed the very thing that might have preserved it. The theater and the entire block it occupied, including the large Pasquale's pizza restaurant on the corner and the longtime home of the WBRC radio studios on the second floor, became a parking lot in the fall of 1982.

Even that was not the end of the story, although unlike that of the Alabama, this one only gets more depressing. While the loss of the Ritz was mostly unmourned, at least one individual seemed to care. He was magician Bill Forstman, who operated a shop known as the Magic Palace in the same block with the Ritz and Pasquale's. When word came down that the wrecking ball was about to begin swinging, Forstman set out to rescue anything he could from the doomed theater. He acquired some of the red leather seats, some advertising films, an usher's uniform and nametag and other artifacts, and he also assembled a scrapbook thoroughly documenting the Ritz's razing in photos. He even purchased two Second Avenue parking meters from the city, just to have more remnants of the old neighborhood.

Forstman made his Magic Palace magically reappear exactly one block south, on First Avenue between Seventeenth and Eighteenth Streets. As part of his new facility, he set up a miniature museum dedicated primarily to his Ritz collection, but also paying tribute to Pasquale's and the other businesses that had been lost in the name of progress.

Unfortunately, Forstman developed some severe health issues that seemed to drain him of his former enthusiasm. His wife reported that for all practical purposes, he lost interest in life long before his passing in 2003. As far as anyone in his family knows, when Forstman locked the doors of the Magic Palace for the last time, the Ritz artifacts were still inside, and they were presumably still there when the aging building was demolished to make room for yet another parking lot. With all the misfortunes the Ritz suffered over its career, the fact that parts of it were indeed preserved, only to be

The Melba Theater opened in March 1946 and was actually the first of the downtown theaters to be originally constructed for sound movies, rather than vaudeville or silent films. This newspaper photo of opening night also shows manager Harry Curl, who went on to run most of the surviving downtown theaters into the early 1980s.

lost in another building's demolition, is tragic in the extreme but perhaps a fitting end.

The theaters we have visited up to this point had one thing in common: all of them were originally constructed for either stage performances or silent movies. It was not until immediately after World War II that downtown Birmingham got its last new movie theater, which also happened to be the first one built specifically for sound films.

The Melba Theatre, as it was eventually named, opened with all the appropriate fanfare on March 14, 1946. Its eastern wall adjoined the towering Comer (later, City Federal) building. Newspapers reported that crowds were stretched double almost the entire length of the block and that "patrons wandered through the lounges and powder room, admiring the restrained modernism of the interior and the luxurious fittings."

Even a relatively new facility like the Melba could not escape the passion for remodeling, and in 1964, the theater received a makeover, giving the interior a color scheme described as turquoise and tangerine, which must have made it resemble an overcrowded Howard Johnson's restaurant. These cosmetic changes were not enough to stop the inevitable passing of time, though.

The decline of the downtown theaters was not really even a gradual slope. In 1969, the Melba, Empire, Alabama and others were still showing the latest Walt Disney films and other family-friendly fare. Just five years later, in 1974, there was not a general audience picture to be seen downtown. Of course, fewer such movies were being produced at all, but as longtime downtown theater manager Harry Curl put it in 1980, "A lot of the movies we show are black oriented, but we show what's available. If we showed general audience movies, we wouldn't attract enough customers to make money. If you've got a good action picture (*Bolo Brute* is now at the Empire) they come in. I don't think they [regular downtown customers] would come to see *Kramer vs. Kramer*."

Curl had a good point. The family movie audience was shrinking in the first place, and those who were still inclined to visit theaters were more likely to do so in the suburbs, such as at the Eastwood Mall Theater that opened in 1964. (Eastwood Mall itself was developed by Henry Waters, who also owned many of the downtown theaters; obviously, Mr. Waters could see where the future was heading long before it got there.)

The same 1980 article that contained Harry Curl's remarks above closed with this observation: "Blacks who do not have the transportation money to see first-run movies at the suburban shopping centers do go to the downtown theaters now. But they are not going in such large numbers that it will never become more feasible to close those theaters."

And that was exactly what happened. Within four years of that article, the Empire and Melba had been demolished, and the Alabama was just beginning its long, torturous process of being preserved. The Ritz was gone, the Lyric had ceased showing pornography and sat abandoned and the other theaters of the past were either parking lots or converted back into retail space. And with that, the day of the downtown movie house faded to black.

Chapter 8

DOWNTOWN'S DEATH AND REBIRTH

So what ultimately happened to kill off downtown as a retail and entertainment source? There is no simple answer to that question. Certainly the decline of Birmingham's downtown was not unique; the older city centers in scores of other communities faced the same problems. (Witness New York City's concentrated effort to revitalize Times Square as a tourist destination, wresting control away from the sleazier elements that had taken it over.) Most of the problems can be traced back to one central fact of life: people went downtown to shop, eat, be entertained by the movies and work, but the vast majority did not live downtown. This especially became the case beginning in the late 1940s, when all those returning war veterans began getting married and producing large families; more often than not, they chose to live in sprawling subdivisions on the far extremities of each city. Therefore, sheer convenience became the first nail in downtown's coffin.

In Birmingham, one of the earliest signs that things were on the move came when the first phase of the eventual mammoth Five Points West Shopping City (originally known as Fairgrounds Shopping Center) opened on U.S. 11 southwest of downtown shortly before World War II. Many of the same businesses that thrived downtown would establish branch stores at Five Points West during the postwar era: W.T. Grant, Woolworth's, Britling, Parisian and, later, Pizitz all located there. Then, in August 1960, the opposite side of town got something no one in Alabama had ever seen before. Eastwood Mall opened with much hoopla as the first enclosed shopping area in the state, and it, too, had its share of tenants who had established themselves downtown first. Just a few years after its opening, Eastwood Mall also built its own movie theater. Clearly, downtown no longer had a monopoly on anything.

Around the same time, discount department stores began to open in the suburbs, and they sapped shoppers from downtown because of not only their convenience but also their lower prices. Bargain Town U.S.A. lured them in with its oft-repeated cha-cha-cha radio and TV jingle, "They buy for less so they can sell for less/The money you save will bring you happiness/That's why people from all over town/Say if you like bargains, you'll love Bargain Town, U.S.A."

In November 1962, the gigantic G*E*S department store opened on Lomb Avenue in West End (and would eventually produce another location in Roebuck). G*E*S was very much the ancestor of today's Walmarts and Costcos. It had a staggering number of departments all under one roof, from groceries to automotive service to a pharmacy and everything imaginable in between. G*E*S was a membership store, as Costco and Sam's Club are today, and one had to have a valid card before shopping there.

Other discount stores were outgrowths of the older, established downtown staples. The Woolco chain was, as the name might suggest, owned by Woolworth's. As mentioned earlier, Kmart was a modernized branch of the venerable S.S. Kresge variety store chain, which had opened a store in Eastwood Mall and other suburban shopping centers. Kmart ended up outlasting G*E*S, Woolco and all the other stores that sprang up during the same period, and the ultimate irony of the retail world occurred when Kmart made the bold move of buying the once-healthy, now-ailing Sears, Roebuck & Co.

While shoppers and moviegoers were being drawn away from downtown, so were those looking to grab a quick bite. Downtown restaurants such as Joy Young and Britling were not usually considered the place for casual attire, and while children were welcome, they were expected to be on their best behavior. Thus, when drive-in restaurants such as the homegrown Jack's Hamburgers, Ed Salem's and Burger in a Hurry began dishing out the grub, many new families created by the baby boom elected to eat at their less elegant surroundings, where it did not matter if Junior spilled his chocolate milkshake and then screamed bloody murder about it.

The transfer of business loyalty from downtown to the suburbs is sometimes referred to as "white flight," but it occurred even in cities that had not undergone Birmingham's bloody experiences during the civil rights

Civil rights demonstrators staged sit-ins at most of the downtown lunch counters during 1962–63. Here, Woolworth's counter seems to be occupied by only two protestors, while the rest of the customers appear to be puzzled by what is going on. Today, this area of the building is a storage room.

movement. Although that social rehab took place over a number of years, actually its direct connection with Birmingham's main theater and retail district amounted to only about four months.

In the spring of 1962, civil rights leaders had tried to promote a boycott of the downtown department stores, but the results were flimsy at best. It was a year later, during the 1963 Easter season, that the movement became more organized, and the resulting loss of business really did hit the stores where it mattered most. The sit-ins at the lunch counters also took place during that spring, and the business owners soon opened negotiations that would bring about an end to segregation. By July, the separate restroom and drinking fountain signs had come down, and the lunch counters were open to one and all. The initial stores participating in this brave new world (which got a certain amount of criticism for doing so) were Loveman's, Pizitz, H.L. Green, S.H. Kress, Britt's and Woolworth's. Sears took the coward's way out

The need for the downtown stores to place their African American employees in more prominent jobs than working the stock room or running elevators was a big part of the 1963 civil rights protests. Although it took a while to complete, by July of that year, the "separate" signs had come down, and progress was certainly visible, if not entirely complete.

by dismantling its restaurant after receiving orders from Chicago to do so; it would be several years before it got a new one.

(Interestingly, far less has been documented as to how the movie theaters and the restaurants such as Joy Young and Britling handled all of this. However, once the stores decided to end segregation, the official laws that had enforced such practices were also repealed, so presumably the restaurants and theaters could do as they pleased afterward.)

Once the retail battle downtown was over, as most people know, attention moved to the issue of school integration that fall and culminated in the bombing of the Sixteenth Street Baptist Church in September. By that time, the downtown business leaders could only shake their heads and wonder why others could not resolve the problems as comparatively easily as they had.

So just when did downtown finally realize it was in danger of losing its prominence as a shopping and entertainment destination? We could trace back through the stories already told here, but when Burger-Phillips closed its downtown store in 1975, no one seemed to attach any particular significance to the event. The other stores dropped off one by one in an escalating number over the next decade or so: S.H. Kress and Odum, Bowers & White in 1978; Loveman's and Joy Young in 1980; Yeilding's in 1981; New Williams in 1983; Blach's, Pizitz (by then McRae's) and Woolworth's in 1988; Sears in 1990; J.J. Newberry in 1995; Parisian in 2007; and Bromberg's in 2009. We have also seen how the movie theaters experienced a dramatic plummet between the late 1960s and mid-1970s. Possibly the symbolic lowest point for the formerly bustling business district was late 1996 and early 1997. At that point, the venerable Downtown Action Committee, a longtime booster of everything from special sales weeks to Christmas celebrations, officially disbanded because there was nothing left to boost.

What does the future hold for Birmingham's downtown theater and retail district? Even its most optimistic backers will be the first to admit that the neighborhood's next life does not include becoming a magnificent shopping district again. Loft apartments became increasingly popular in the first few years of the twenty-first century, and even though such development was temporarily crippled by the 2008 recession, developers have now picked up their plans and are moving forward once again. There is always the hope that more people living downtown will spur retail, food and entertainment projects to take root, but certainly not in the form with which the area is still identified in people's memories.

When the original version of this manuscript was written in 2004, loft development had barely gotten started, and it was somewhat difficult to know just how it was going to affect the long-vacant downtown buildings. The closing paragraph of that first draft read:

> *There are still relics of downtown's past for those who care to look for them. Signage for many of the long-closed businesses can still be found clinging to the stores' carcasses. Many logos are still inset into the marble or terra-cotta forecourts of the department stores. However, if redevelopment does come, these elements will not be preserved as part of the buildings' new usages. When the last of them is painted over, paved over, ripped up or otherwise demolished, that will truly be the end of the story of downtown Birmingham as we know it, and all that will be left will be the memories of people old enough to have experienced the district in its glory days. About forty years from now, even those individuals will be gone, and whatever face downtown is wearing by that time will be considered the one it has always had.*

We can all breathe a sigh of relief that my dire predictions did not come true, or at least not nearly as much as the above Gloomy Gus pronouncement would indicate. Before we reach our last page, we will take a look at some of the buildings that have played such a prominent role in this story and see how their health is holding up in old age.

Our first chapter was all about Pizitz and Loveman's, and the fates of two major department store buildings could not be more diametrically opposed. As has been mentioned several times, ten years after Loveman's final customer walked through the doors, the city of Birmingham made arrangements to purchase the building as the home for a science museum. It would be a merger of two smaller local museums, the Discovery Place and the Red Mountain Museum, and the proposed name was Discovery 2000. Since it quickly became apparent that this name was going to become outdated sooner rather than later, by the time the museum opened in 1998, it had become the McWane Science Center. The museum utilizes all of Loveman's former selling space except the fourth floor, and great pains were taken to preserve the many Loveman's artifacts that were still scattered throughout. The beautiful marble work around the elevators was restored to its 1935 art deco appearance, even though the beloved escalators had to be removed and replaced with conventional stairs. The McWane Science Center is one of Birmingham's top attractions, and even those too young to have ever seen Loveman's in its prime can be impressed by the sheer magnitude of their surroundings.

In stark contrast, the Pizitz building has been allowed to molder and decay ever since its closing in early 1988. There have been several attempts to reverse the rot, beginning in October 2000, when two days of former Pizitz employee reunions were held on the main floor. After that, things seemed to progress jerkily. The owner, Bayer Properties, was all set to develop Pizitz into an office complex by 2010. But then the recession worsened, and the biggest potential occupants dropped out. In 2013, plans were revived, this time to turn the abandoned hulk into loft apartments, with retail space at street level. As of this writing, it is too soon to tell whether this will finally be Pizitz's happy ending or just another dashed hope.

(As with Loveman's, many relics were left inside when the store closed. Interestingly, virtually everything still bears the Pizitz name, not McRae's, a somewhat telling clue that when McRae's bought out the company, it never really intended to make the downtown store a permanent part of the chain.)

As for the Blach's building, its eventual rehabilitation was a bit more unusual in that it had also been a hotel before the store ever moved into it and had been the original Yeilding's store even before that. From 1988 until 2005, it sat vacant, with the white paint peeling off the exterior. Once the project to convert the store-turned-hotel-turned-store-turned-eyesore into fifteen loft apartments began, the construction crew began uncovering evidence of all the various phases of the building's former lives.

As with most of these projects, the primary historical preservation would be on the exterior. All of the old downtown buildings had a plethora of features that would render them uninhabitable for present-day tenants, including copious amounts of asbestos and lead-based paint. For that reason, projects such as the one at Blach's involved literally tearing everything out, down to the bare concrete, and beginning anew. During this process at Blach's, the newspapers reported:

> *So far, crews working on the building have found everything from old bottles to mirrors to the mechanical parts of the old freight elevator complete with a giant wheel, cables and pulleys. The demolition has also uncovered old fireplaces behind the walls and other features from when the building housed the 100-room Bencor Hotel. Work on the mezzanine uncovered a beautiful plaster tray ceiling with crown molding that appears to have covered the hotel lobby.*

Unlike the prediction made a decade ago, the Blach's "Fair and Square" emblem inlaid into the terrazzo floors was not ripped up or covered over, but preserved as an important historic sight. Also, like several other such

The process of converting former downtown stores into offices and loft apartments sometimes revealed hidden surprises. This damaged but elaborate sign inside the former Burger-Phillips store was one of those.

development projects, the Blach's Lofts continue to use the same lettering style and black-and-white motif as the store's logo, providing more than a little sense of continuity.

A similar project began at the nearby Burger-Phillips building in 2008. Trying to maintain some links to the past was a little more difficult there, because instead of having sat vacant since the closing in 1975, Burger-Phillips had received at least one makeover during its brief career as part of the Costa-Head plan. Getting rid of its 1980s look was one of the first steps in converting it into the Burger-Phillips Lofts (again, using the same logo as the store). One of the most impressive revelations was an enormous bas-relief sign over the former main entrance, depicting an elegantly attired lady with the caption, "Famous for Fashions Since 1895." The piece was likely created when Burger-Phillips moved into the building in 1933, but there is always the possibility it could have been something the firm brought with it from the earlier location.

Now, let's talk about the various Parisian buildings left over from that beloved retailer's migration throughout downtown. As was detailed earlier, the enormous store at the corner of Third Avenue and Eighteenth Street served many different occupants after Parisian's forced exit. When we last left it, the building was serving as one of A.G. Gaston's flagship offices, housing first his bank and later his insurance company. Eventually, even Gaston's enterprises pulled out and the structure—which no one could reasonably be expected to remember as having once been Parisian—was left empty once more. In the summer of 2013, efforts began to convert it into (here they are again) either upscale loft apartments or office space.

The longest-serving Parisian store, the one on Second Avenue North that formerly hosted the Caheen Brothers, as of this writing has remained vacant, with an interesting mix of styles visible. The terrazzo entrance still bears the inlaid Parisian logo of the 1940s and 1950s, while the doors are decorated with signage dating to 1989, when Parisian vacated the premises. A remodeling program of unknown vintage, but probably from the early 1980s, has covered the art deco–inspired façade with some odd stone or gravel-like walls. Should renovation ever reach this one, removal of that look should be among the first things to be done, as it really seems out of place among the other Second Avenue structures. As for the final Parisian downtown location in the Regions Harbert Plaza, after Belk abandoned it, the prime property became, somewhat unusually, an upscale gym for those downtown workers who wanted to build muscle during their lunch breaks instead of stuffing their faces.

With so many of the former stores serving purposes so far afield from their original functions, perhaps we should take comfort that the former Odum, Bowers & White store has continued to operate as a clothing store. The building was not allowed to sit vacant for long after the fancy-pants clothier sold its last suit, and it has been known as Jean's Glory since then. It may not be as exclusive, but along with the Alabama Theatre, it seems to be at least trying to maintain some semblance of its former life.

Two of the other clothing stores, New Williams and New Ideal, have found themselves in the same situation as the Second Avenue Parisian. Both have been empty for years, although, at least for a while, the New Williams building was home to a cosmetology school. Both are rather sad sights now, but there is always the hope that some developer will succeed in bringing them back to life. The interior of New Ideal still contains much of the signage and decoration from its operating days, although a trip up to the mezzanine can be a bit creepy; dozens of discarded nude mannequins lie strewn about like victims of a mass murder, their sightless eyes staring at the ceiling as if wondering what happened to them.

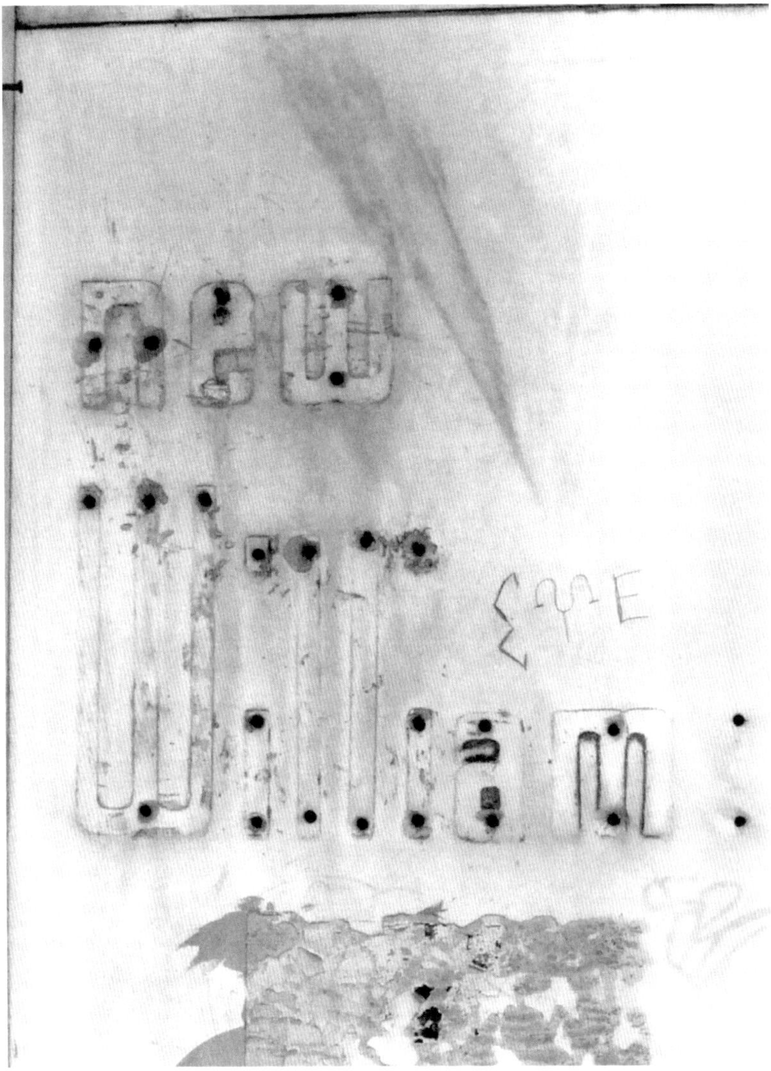

Some of the abandoned buildings downtown still await some sort of renovation. This scar on the pink marble exterior is all that remains to memorialize longtime women's clothier New Williams.

Yeilding's, as we saw, immediately became the new location for Calder Furniture once the farm-store-turned-women's-clothing-store closed in 1981. Since Calder went on to wherever former furniture stores go, Yeilding's has also remained empty, awaiting the next big idea to come its way.

Fortunately, even though Bromberg's chose to close the downtown store in 2009, one would never know it. Since the company headquarters are housed there, and the windows are kept cheery with displays of Bromberg's high-end merchandise, those walking or driving past would be hard-pressed to even realize the store was no longer open. An intriguing remnant of Bromberg's former reputation as a camera center can be found in one of the Second Avenue entrance bays, where a small metal drop box labeled FILM can still be seen, a reminder of the store's once-busy photo processing service.

In the realm of the five-and-ten-cent stores, of course, absolutely nothing remains to memorialize the J.J. Newberry building. When it was demolished to make way for the McWane Science Center's IMAX Theater, the job was certainly a thorough one. Newberry's variety store neighbors fared somewhat better. After the S.H. Kress building emerged from the long shadow cast by the Costa-Head project, it was leased to the federal government for a variety of offices. The feds had packed up their dark glasses and secret weapons by 2003, and Kress began yet another life as the headquarters for the Wiggins, Childs, Quinn and Pantazis law firm. Today, even the basement (where the toy department and the 1960s sit-ins lunch counter were) has found a new reputation as the home to a theater group. Through all the various tenants, the shiny gold Kress signs on the exterior have been lovingly preserved, although the red neon letters on the flagpole were removed long ago; only some telltale metal patches indicate where they used to be.

After Woolworth's closed at the end of 1988, entrepreneur David Kim moved into the space with his California Fashion Mall. Primarily selling inexpensive women's apparel, wigs and costume jewelry, it has a different character than Woolworth's ever did, but not drastically. Inside, the walls and beautiful terrazzo floors (now somewhat cracked) look about the same, and the Woolworth's emblem, a red W within a diamond shape, can still be found in front of each entrance. Kim recalls that when he first moved into the building, the historic lunch counter and its stools were still in place, but he converted that area into a storage room, and the only remaining evidence of the lunch counter is, surprisingly, the kitchen and the window through which the prepared meals would be passed to the waitresses tending the hungry horde.

As we have already seen, when S.H. Kress left its Second Avenue building for the gleaming new edifice on Third Avenue, fellow variety store veteran W.T. Grant had soon taken over its former abode. Over the years, though, Grant's never required as much space as Kress had, so only about two-thirds of the ex-Kress were part of the deal. (The remaining third became Burt's

Shoes, among other lessees.) Grant's left downtown in early 1973, and by that summer, much of its space had become Snow's Cards and Gifts. Layers of modernization piled up on the front of the building over the decades, but when it was removed, there was Grant's trademark orange and blue color scheme and some barely readable signage with the chain's simple slogan, "Known for Values." At various times, different plans for reviving the former Kress/Grant's store have been presented, but for now it sits empty.

Turning our attention to the restaurants, all of the original downtown locations of the Britling Cafeterias have now been leveled. Some of the suburban buildings do survive in highly remodeled form. After Joy Young closed in September 1980, the building most immediately became a political headquarters during that fall's presidential election. After that, not much happened until most of that block was demolished to make way for the 1986 construction of the SouthTrust bank tower (later Wachovia, now Wells Fargo, and who knows what other bank names in the future).

There is not a lot left to say about the movie theaters. Other than the notable rescue of the Alabama and the ongoing renovations at the Lyric, every other major theater downtown was eventually razed, more often than not to make more parking spaces. There are two exceptions to the rule, relics of the silent movie era that managed to survive in disguises that not even Clark Kent could see through.

On Third Avenue, the Rialto had spent most of the years since the 1930s as a clothing and shoe store. In 2005, a young married couple, Chad and Chesney Moore, obtained the former Rialto and set to work turning the ground floor into a showroom for their office furniture business and the upper floors into living space. As layers of remodeling were removed, evidence of the Rialto's auditorium emerged from hiding, particularly the vaulted ceiling and an unmistakable scar on the walls showing where the balcony had once been attached.

The other camouflaged silent picture house stands on Second Avenue, adjoining the old Kress/Grant's building. Once known as the Trianon, it too left show business soon after the movies began to talk. To judge from photos and the inlaid logo in front of its door, the ex-Trianon spent many years as an outlet of the Peggy Hale women's clothing chain. Currently it is a video store, and while the owners maintain there is nothing remaining from the Trianon era, there is no way to predict what might be found someday if the building is gutted and its theatrical roots happen to begin showing once more.

Possibly no renovation project could rival what became of the Sears building. When we left that famous retailer many pages ago, the windows and

Converting the long-closed Sears store into today's Innovation Depot removed virtually any trace of the building's former life. This photo, taken just as renovations were about to begin, shows one of the surviving 1941 signs mounted over what was once an exit, which had been unceremoniously sealed with concrete blocks to keep out vagrants.

doors had been sealed with cement blocks to keep out unwanted intruders, and the interior was left to decay. Probably everyone thought Sears's useful life was over, but then in late 2005, suddenly there was movement to try to open the sarcophagus and reanimate the corpse inside.

It was announced that the Sears building would be converted into the Innovation Depot, a business incubation center with ties to UAB. As with the other downtown renovations, this meant that virtually everything left from the Sears era would be stripped away, and in this case, that was quite a lot. The initial teams sent in to analyze the building found most of the signage, carpet and fixtures just as they had been on the day the store closed some fifteen years earlier. Some of it even dated back to 1941, such as the once illuminated signs over the sealed-up doors, still indicating "To First Avenue," "To Second Avenue," "To Parking Lot" and so on.

There were initial plans to preserve some of these elements and incorporate them into the Innovation Depot, but while in storage, they mysteriously disappeared. Interestingly, shortly after the Innovation Depot's opening in April 2007, Birmingham's well-known Culinard cooking school decided to open a restaurant in the Innovation Depot, both as a way to serve those who worked there and as on-the-job training for its students. The new Culinard Café would occupy the same spot that had been Sears's 1970 Coffee Shop, a truly coincidental comeback for one of the building's fondly remembered features. Now, if they could only bring back the candy counter, with the chocolate-covered raisins and salted cashews.

So, there you have it, friends and neighbors, a look at how downtown once was and how it is today. This cannot really be considered "the end" because the tale is continuing to unfold every day. With all the changes that have taken place in the decade since the first version of this manuscript, perhaps we should all agree to meet here again—under the clock at Loveman's, where else?—ten years from now and see what is going on in this once vibrant, once decayed, now reviving district.

BIBLIOGRAPHY

Books

Atkins, Leah Rawls. *The Valley and the Hills: An Illustrated History of Birmingham and Jefferson County*. Woodland Hills, CA: Windsor Publications, 1981.

Baggett, James L. *Historic Photos of Birmingham*. Nashville, TN: Turner Publishing, 2006.

Barton, Jessica L. *Historic Photos of Birmingham in the '50s, '60s and '70s*. Nashville, TN: Turner Publishing, 2010.

Bennett, James R. *Blach's: The Store, the Family, Their Story*. Memphis, TN: TVA Publishing Co., 2013.

Century Plus: A Bicentennial Portrait of Birmingham, Alabama. Birmingham, AL: Oxmoor Press, 1976.

Hollis, Tim. *Birmingham's Theater and Retail District*. Charleston, SC: Arcadia Publishing, 2005.

———. *Loveman's: Meet Me Under the Clock*. Charleston, SC: The History Press, 2012.

———. *Pizitz: Your Store*. Charleston, SC: The History Press, 2010.

———. *Vintage Birmingham Signs*. Charleston, SC: The Arcadia Publishing, 2007.

Keith, Todd. *Birmingham Then and Now*. San Diego, CA: Thunder Bay Press, 2008.

King, Pamela Sterne. *50 Years and Counting: A History of Operation New Birmingham*. Birmingham, AL: Operation New Birmingham, 2008.

Lewis, Pierce, and Marjorie Longenecker White. *Birmingham View: Through the Years in Photographs*. Birmingham, AL: Birmingham Historical Society, 1996.

McMillan, Malcolm C. *Yesterday's Birmingham*. Miami, FL: E.A. Seemann Publishing, 1975.

O'Donnell, Joe. *The Forge: Metal to Medicine*. Birmingham, AL: Regional Chamber of Commerce, 2007.

Pitrone, Jean Maddern. *F.W. Woolworth and the American Five and Dime*. Jefferson, NC: McFarland & Co., 2003.

Plunkett-Powell, Karen. *Remembering Woolworth's: A Nostalgic History of the World's Most Famous Five-and-Dime*. New York: St. Martin's Press, 1999.

Portrait of Birmingham. Birmingham, AL: Birmingham Centennial Corporation, 1971.

Sher, David, and Martin Sher. *Collect Debts and Still Keep Your Customers*. New York: American Management Association, 1999.

Smith, J. Morgan. *Bromberg's: An Alabama Tradition for 150 Years*. Birmingham, AL: Southern University Press, 1987.

Thomas, Bernice L. *America's 5 & 10 Cent Stores: The Kress Legacy*. New York: John Wiley & Sons, 1997.

White, Marjorie Longenecker. *Downtown Birmingham*. Birmingham, AL: Birmingham Historical Society, 1977.

Whitmire, Cecil, and Jeannie Hanks. *The Alabama Theatre: Showplace of the South*. Birmingham, AL: Birmingham Landmarks, Inc., 2002.

Wilkinson, Susan, and Hank Griffith. *A Guide to the Building Records of S.H. Kress & Co*. Washington, D.C.: National Building Museum, 1993.

Newspaper & Magazine Articles

Archibald, John. "City Buys Newberry Site for Science Museum Facility." *Birmingham News*, April 14, 1992.

———. "Downtown Action Committee Dies of Inaction." *Birmingham News*, January 15, 1997.

Atkins, Leah Rawls. "The End of an Era Nears." *Birmingham News*, July 29, 2007.

Bell, Elma. "Son of Alabama Theatre Organist Fondly Recalls His Own Days Backstage." *Birmingham News*, August 27, 1991.

Birmingham Chamber of Commerce Newsletter. "The Britling, Where 5,000 Persons Daily are Served, An Indispensable Institution of Birmingham." April 1927.

Birmingham News. "Acme Plans New Theater." Undated clipping.

———. "All Birmingham Invited to Event." April 26, 1925.

———. "Bigger, Brighter New Ideal Opens Thursday." October 19, 1966.
———. "Big New Britt's Opens Downtown." December 3, 1962.
———. "Britling's to Open Third Cafeteria Here." October 14, 1925.
———. "Bromberg's to Be City Showplace." July 21, 1946.
———. "Burger-Phillips Will Close." June 10, 1975.
———. "Downtown Theaters' Post-War Baby, Melba, Sporting Complete New Look." December 25, 1966.
———. "Empire, New Wise Theater, to Open Friday." January 16, 1927.
———. "Formal Dedication of Store Arranged." March 4, 1933.
———. "Grant Company Store to Open Here." September 26, 1930.
———. "Hines' Performance Superb during Temple's Final Show." April 1, 1970.
———. "Ideal Store to Build Six-Story Structure." January 5, 1928.
———. "In Days before the Talkies, Live Theater Flourished." December 19, 1971.
———. "Interior of Ritz Theater Being Torn Up for Cinerama." June 3, 1962.
———. "Magic Doors That Open as Customer Approaches Featured at Burger-Phillips." November 8, 1936.
———. "Montgomery Ward Enlarges Store to Better Serve Birmingham Folk." August 14, 1930.
———. "New Belk-Hudson Store Will Open Early Next Month." January 23, 1955.
———. "New Ideal to Move March 1." January 15, 1942.
———. "New Playhouse for Birmingham to Cost Million." Undated clipping.
———. "New Store to Be Host in Reception." August 16, 1931.
———. "New Structure Brings Fifth Avenue Here." September 12, 1937.
———. "New Williams Is Recession Victim." January 12, 1983.
———. "O.B.W. Presents Shiny New Store to City." September 6, 1948.
———. "Odum, Bowers Store to Close in the Fall." May 8, 1978.
———. "Old Culture Gives Way to Progress." January 5, 1950.
———. "$100,000 Remodeling Job Slated for Empire." August 9, 1964.
———. "Parisian Company Ready in Their New Home." August 29, 1933.
———. "Parisian's Downtown Store Unveils Remodeled Face." October 22, 1950.
———. "Parisian to Take Additional Space." May 14, 1939.
———. "Personal Touch Walgreen Idea." January 20, 1940.
———. "Playhouse Will Open within Year on Second Avenue." September 27, 1925.
———. "Ritz, Million Dollar Theater, Opens Monday with New York Bill." August 16, 1926.

———. "Sears Modern New Store Here Will Have Its Formal Opening." October 12, 1941.

———. "Third Avenue, 18th Street Building Bought by Calder Furniture Co." January 6, 1946.

———. "Woolworth's Moves into New Three-Story Home." Undated clipping.

———. "Yeilding Brothers to Spend $250,000 Remodeling." Undated clipping.

———. "Yeilding Closes Last Two Stores over Weekend." December 30, 1996.

Birmingham Post. "Empire Has Permastone Face Lifting." November 2, 1949.

———. "Kress Company Firm Obtains Blach's Site for Edifice." November 20, 1935.

———. "Melancon's Green Star Rises after Deliberation." September 26, 1933.

———. "Melba Theater Has the Latest of Everything." March 13, 1946.

———. "New Theater Is Packed for Opening Show." March 15, 1946.

———. "Parisian to Leave Its Old Location." July 6, 1933.

Birmingham Post-Herald. "Britling's on First Avenue to Close Doors Today." October 17, 1964.

———. "Life of Blach's Spans 160 Years." March 8, 1963.

———. "Newmar Theater Takes over Strand." Undated clipping.

Brown, Tommy. "The Grande Dame of Theaters Relives." *Birmingham News*, October 11, 1980.

Bryant, Joseph D. "City Funds Study to Restore Lyric Theatre." *Birmingham News*, November 5, 2005.

Carter, Lane. "Golden Age of Theater Recalled." *Birmingham News*, December 11, 1960.

———. "Old Strand Will Always Stand If Only in Reporter's Memory." *Birmingham News*, August 2, 1963.

———. "Temple's Curtain Goes Down Tonight." *Birmingham News*, March 31, 1970.

———. "Temple Theater: Soon a Memory." *Birmingham News Magazine*, November 9, 1969.

Chandler, Lori. "Old Blach's Building Could Play Pivotal Role." *Birmingham News*, March 17, 2002.

Childress, Mark. "Kress' Final Closing to End Era." *Birmingham News*, January 8, 1978.

Crowe, Bill. "Some Joy Leaving Birmingham." *Birmingham News*, April 27, 1980.

Dalrymple, Dolly. "Birmingham Gets $1,500,000 Christmas Present." *Birmingham News*, December 25, 1927.

———. "Herman Saks and Sons Celebrate Their First Anniversary in New Second Avenue Store." *Birmingham News*, March 28, 1926.

———. "New Ritz Manager, Veteran of Movie Game, Says Changes Only Sure Thing." *Birmingham News*, March 25, 1931.

Diel, Stan. "Civic Leader Hess Is Dead; Left a Legacy." *Birmingham News*, August 2, 1996.

Ferguson, Hill. "Golden Days of Bijou Recalled." *Birmingham Post*, May 4, 1950.

Gordon, Tom. "Remembering Downtown." *Birmingham News*, May 12, 1991.

Harvey, Alec. "Alabama Theatre Growing; Takes on Additional Space." *Birmingham News*, November 22, 1992.

———. "Cecil Whitmire Dies." *Birmingham News*, August 23, 2010.

———. "The Mighty Cecil Retires from the Wurlitzer." *Birmingham News*, August 28, 2007.

Horne, Terry. "Million-dollar Ritz Faces $50,000 Demolition." *Birmingham Post-Herald*, September 22, 1982.

Huebner, Michael. "Renovation of Lyric Theatre Turns Serious." *Birmingham News*, September 14, 2003.

Huie, William R. "Mickey Mousers Are Good Citizens." *Birmingham News*, undated clipping.

Ingram, Charlie. "Organ Society Seeks to Buy Alabama Theatre, Needs $100,000." *Birmingham News*, March 12, 1987.

Jackson, Harold. "Story of Ritz Mirrors Change in Downtown." *Birmingham Post-Herald*, January 10, 1980.

Keith, Walling. "Closed Strand Tugs Heart." *Birmingham News*, December 3, 1962.

———. "Where Old Bijou Stood." *Birmingham News*, April 22, 1965.

Kent, Dawn. "Belk Plans to Close Store Downtown." *Birmingham News*, August 1, 2008.

———. "Downtown Belk Marks Its Last Christmas Eve." *Birmingham News*, December 25, 2008.

———. "Former High-end Store to Convert to Lofts, Retail." *Birmingham News*, February 7, 2008.

———. "Get Ready, Get Set, Grow!" *Birmingham News*, April 19, 2007.

LaCross, Nova. "Museum Holds Ritz Memories." *Birmingham News*, undated clipping.

Mahoney, Ryan. "Law Firm Buys Burger-Phillips Centre." *Birmingham Business Journal*, May 23, 2003.

Matthews, Susan. "Seen Better Days, but Lyric on Historic List." *Birmingham News*, July 15, 1977.

Meredith, Depew. "Parking Lot Will Replace Old Jefferson." *Birmingham Post*, August 12, 1946.

Metro Magazine. "Lyric Theatre Had Checkered Past." November 8, 1978.

Pratt, Ted. "Aland's Joining List of Closed Retail Stores." *Birmingham News*, January 5, 1997.

———. "Yeilding to Shut Stores after 120 Years in City." *Birmingham News*, October 6, 1996.

Reeves, Garland. "Great Alabama Theatre Battles to Keep Afloat." *Birmingham News*, February 12, 1978.

Ruisi, Anne. "Five-and-Dime Era Comes to End as Woolworth's Stores Close." *Birmingham News*, November 2, 1997.

Rynecki, David. "Downtown Birmingham's Retail Bust." *Birmingham News*, December 20, 1994.

Shatz, Howard. "Empire Bows Out." *Birmingham News*, July 17, 1984.

Shook, Phil H. "New Williams Will Open Again." *Birmingham News*, May 25, 1980.

———. "Yeilding's to Close, Calder's to Lease." *Birmingham News*, January 4, 1981.

Shorey, Kenneth Paul. "Farewell to Bijou and Centennial Cinemas." *Birmingham News*, April 14, 1974.

Tomberlin, Michael. "Belk Buys Parisian." *Birmingham News*, August 3, 2006.

———. "Blach's Back in High Style." *Birmingham News*, November 21, 2004.

———. "Blach's Renovation Reveals Treasures." *Birmingham News*, January 21, 2005.

———. "Building Future on City's Past." *Birmingham News*, May 23, 2004.

———. "Burger-Phillips Centre Has New Ownership." *Birmingham News*, October 19, 2001.

———. "Change for Kress." *Birmingham News*, October 19, 2003.

———. "Downtown Parisian to Get $7.5m Facelift." *Birmingham News*, September 1, 2013.

———. "Dull Downtown Sites to Shine." *Birmingham News*, July 23, 2006.

———. "Innovation Depot New Name of Incubator." *Birmingham News*, May 13, 2006.

Underwood, Madison. "A Sign of New Times for the Lyric." *Birmingham News*, September 29, 2013.

Weaver, Emmett. "Strand Theater Ends Nearly 50-Year Run." *Birmingham Post-Herald*, November 29, 1962.

———. "Two Old-Film Buffs Restore the Lyric." *Birmingham Post-Herald*, April 18, 1973.

Whetstone, Joe. "Samford to Hang Temple Theater's Huge Chandelier." *Birmingham News*, April 17, 1970.

Williams, Roy L. "Closing after Eight Decades." *Birmingham News*, January 25, 1995.

———. "Downtown Loses a Gem: Bromberg's Store Closes." *Birmingham News*, March 7, 2009.

———. "On the Record: Mae Rosenberger." *Birmingham News*, May 8, 2005.

———. "Walls to Fall: Newberry's Will Make Way for Theater." *Birmingham News*, March 8, 1996.

ABOUT THE AUTHOR

Tim Hollis has been a pop culture historian literally all his life. He likes to tell how when he was nine years old, he was writing letters to companies and trying to preserve the memories of things from when he was three years old. This mania for living in the past has resulted in twenty-three books (as of right now, anyway), ranging in subjects from southern tourism nostalgia to Birmingham history to children's television and children's records, among other topics. He also owns a museum of toys, advertising, holiday memorabilia and other baby-boomer relics that he makes available to visitors and researchers by appointment. Having lived in Birmingham his entire life, he supplies the nostalgic materials for the popular www.BirminghamRewound.com website, through which he may also be contacted.

Visit us at
www.historypress.net

This title is also available as an e-book